THE DARING DANE

The Dream of Peter Lassen,
the Man from Farum

Elisabeth Lyneborg

VANTAGE PRESS
New York / Atlanta
Los Angeles / Chicago

Also by Elisabeth Lyneborg

Præster er osse mennesker (Parsons Are Also Human Beings)
Det spøger i stalden (The Stable Is Haunted)
Jeg var der (I Was There)
Regnbuekrigeren (The Rainbow Warrior)
Den blåu kat (The Blue Cat)

FIRST EDITION

All rights reserved, including the right of reproduction in whole or in part in any form.

Copyright © 1988 by Elisabeth Lyneborg

Published by Vantage Press, Inc.
516 West 34th Street, New York, New York 10001

Manufactured in the United States of America
ISBN: 0-533-07614-5

Library of Congress Catalog Card No.: 87-90216

Preface

Opposite the Farum city hall, in a green area on the other side of Frederiksborgvej, stands an unimpressive obelisk in black granite.

On the polished slab, it reads:

> The Dane Peter Lassen of California (USA)
> Born in Farum 31 October 1800
> Died in California 26 April 1859
> Denmark and the USA honor his memory

Nobody takes any particular notice of this memorial. Few at Farum, or in Denmark for that matter, know who Peter Lassen was. In California, several localities are named after him: streets, rivers, a national park and, last but not least, the volcano Mount Lassen or Lassen Peak. For a period he was the president of a North Californian republic.

It is difficult to give an adequate characterization of a person. It will always be just a few brush strokes on a far-larger painting.

Every individual is a boundless and enigmatic universe. That is why we are always both-this-and-that people.

My most important source for this book is T. Vogel-Jørgensen's *Peter Lassen of California* from 1937.

However, my book should not be regarded as a historical novel about Peter Lassen's fantastic fate.

On the contrary, the book reflects the dream that Peter Lassen's life history has created in myself.

The Daring Dane

In his hour of death, the lobe of a Danish beech leaf had brushed his mind, but he died with both hands buried deep in the Californian soil.

One

Down at Lake Farum, the autumn gale flapped the branches of the trees vigorously, while the full moon looked on disinterestedly.

In a little thatched house not far from the lake, a young woman struggled through her labor pains. The air in the dark alcove was heavy with suffering. She distinctly felt the hard bottom boards against her tailbone, for the straw bedding was thin and old. The delivery had commenced a whole month earlier than she had reckoned, so nothing was ready for the baby.

With thin red-blotched hands she clasped the striped edge of the eiderdown. Now and again she let go her grasp, and her hands crawled like homeless crabs over the cover. When new throes set in, they scurried back frightened to their first position.

Johanne was alone in the small simple room. There was little furniture: a small plank table, a wooden bench with a shelf above it, on which three English faience plates had been neatly placed. On one plate, a drake appeared on a delicate light-blue background. On the second, a pheasant could be seen by a low green bush on a somewhat darker blue background. But the third plate was slightly different in firing and subject, for on that one a windmill was depicted in three shades of blue.

There was no curtain at the small lopsided rustic window. Something quite unusual for such an indigent room hung next to it on the wall—a clock, a fine clock in a handsome wooden case, with a carved column on either side. The dial was white with Roman numerals, and behind the glass pane the pendulum swung back and forth in restless motion, telling something about time. Time, elapsing indifferently, races man and generations across life and death, across the earth and all that belongs to the earth, held in place by its gravitation. One day when no one can measure time any longer, it will ransack the marshalling yard of the universe in solitary spirals.

On the plank table, a tallow candle flickered in the draft from the little window and from the crooked door, which had long since given up reaching down to the worn threshold. The door led out onto a short cobbled passage, which ended in a transversely divided door.

In front of the house lay a grass field. The grass was halfgrown and suffered from fall fatigue. It yielded readily to the strong wind, while the silver sheen of the moon caressed it on both sides. Sometimes the white dream-field disappeared in a gloomy darkness when the moon glided behind a threatening autumn cloud.

But Lake Farum led its own nightlife, indifferent to the events occurring in the little thatched house up there in the field. The naked boughs stretched out over the black waters of the lake that whispered in introspective search. The lake was sure to know—for it had seen and heard before. It had dreamed and murmured in the summer night, roared in the autumn storm, become silent during the frost under the heavy ice, and gurgled delightedly with the first mild springtime wind.

Nature turns away from the doings of human beings. Still, that is how it was at the time—things have changed since then, unfortunately. Now, many years later, long after Johanne struggled through her pangs in the little thatched house near Lake Farum, Nature can no longer turn away. For now Man has made himself the master! Now the lake can no longer dream in happy awareness of itself. Now fish and bird can no longer freely imbibe water and air, for Man has used all his knowledge to destroy the very Nature that has given him the fortune, vigor, and strength to do all that his heart has secretly longed for. He has developed a technology with which to govern, but just like Nature, that technology wants its own thing, and therefore, as elsewhere, the spark of life has disappeared from Lake Farum.

At that time, in the year 1800, on October 31 to be exact, the world was still its old self.

An old nag hitched to a small lopsided carriage struggled through the storm. Lars Nielsen was seated on the box, and next to him dangled a stunted woman. With one hand she clung to Lars, and with the other she tried to keep together the black shawl that she had wrapped around her shoulders and head—her bony hand holding the shawl together under her pointed chin.

It was blowing a gale, it was cold, and the clouds drifted along hastily. Each time a cloud passed the moon, the silvery light returned benevolently to the landscape. There was a sorcerous power in the moonlight, a strength and an unrest in this strange gleam from the underworld.

The fetal fluid had passed and seeped out into the flattened straw bedding. Johanne gasped. She had given up hope that Lars would arrive in time with the midwife. She was clinging to the large wet eiderdown in pain and resignation.

Even though the air was raw, she had thrown her legs around the eiderdown and held it fast as if it were a log she was climbing. Barely twenty-four, Johanne was well acquainted with resignation. What cannot be changed cannot be helped.

She had given birth before; eighteen months ago she had Johan. Fortunately, he was at Herlev these days with her father, the schoolmaster and parish clerk.

The last delivery was bad, but she had managed for she had had hope. Lars was with her during the entire delivery. Her mother and the midwife had also been there. Johanne had been looking forward to giving birth. She had believed in the whole occurrence, and in Lars and herself as parents. Now her long fair hair was greasy and her skin gray. She was not young any longer. She was not in love with Lars and she was not sure that she cared to live with him at all. But she knew that she must.

Her father, the parish clerk, had been furious when she had taken an unskilled laborer—a day laborer. Meanwhile, Johanne had decided to take Lars because she had believed that they were sure to get something out of a life together. Now she knew it was impossible. Lars could never get anything done. Lars could never get off on time. He could easily make the day go by doing nothing. He never noticed when dusk came creeping.

Meanwhile Johanne toiled and moiled and tried to cook food from well nigh nothing. Lars could not pull himself together to seek employment.

She was so tired now and no longer felt like doing anything. She moaned, and another labor pain made her lose her breath. She relaxed the hold of her legs on the eiderdown, let go of it between her knees, and looked down. The eiderdown was wet and smeared with bloody slime.

Through the gale she heard the distant sound of a carriage rumbling in the ruts down toward the house. *Hopefully he has Marie, the midwife, with him*, she thought wearily.

Soon after, the outer door opened, and the gale reached into the living room and the candle on the table. The door to the room slammed wide open and struck against the wall. Lars carried Marie in.

He hurried out again and closed both doors. He had to take the old nag into the outhouse. The horse was not his own. He borrowed it from the next-door neighbor, who was not very keen on lending it. "You can only have it for today and only because Johanne needs Marie," the neighbor had said in a sullen tone. Lars often asked himself why people liked Johanne and shunned him. Marie stood there in the middle of the room, shuddering. "Have you got a dram?" she called toward the bed. Johanne moaned and pointed with a blotchy hand to the kitchen corner.

"Ugh, how dark and cold it is here," mumbled Marie, putting the shawl away on the table. At lightning speed she found the aquavit, took a swig of the bottle, and put it over by the cold fireplace. Then she wobbled across to Johanne, whose fingers she disengaged rather harshly so that she might pull off the eiderdown. "O Lord! The child is almost out," she whinnied, startled. "Where is that slothful scamp of Lars? Well, there he comes. There now, get the fire lit and let us have some hot water to bathe your offspring. To be sure, you haven't been loath to make it; but of course you're gone when the brat arrives."

Lars had come inside. Somewhat taken aback, he took off his cap and removed a few autumn leaves that have stuck in the grayish wool. He put on his cap again and at a slow pace set about lighting the fireplace with the last two logs at hand. He poured water from the pail into the pot. Meanwhile, Marie moved around cursing and swearing at this godforsaken house, where nothing of any kind was to be found.

"You must have some swaddling clothes or something," she groused. Marie then grabbed the tallow candle off the table and placed it on a chair next to the alcove.

Johanne moaned with pain. Her happiness and debasement had been reached. Here she lay in her hard box bed with her knees pulled all up, with her head high, the back of her neck strained to the utmost, and her chin pressed down against her chest in a long, helpless, creaking breath, while her womb spewed water and blood. The hard ball pressed outward and dropped onto the flattened straw at the bottom of the box bed.

"O Lord," cried Marie from the fireplace, where she had just taken a gulp to keep warm and stay in high spirits. "You can never have peace and quiet anywhere, can you?" With both her unwashed hands, she seized the little greasy lump at the bottom of the bed. She straightened it out, lifted it by the tiny thin legs, and swung it back and forth. "It's a boy. Get your jaws opened, lad. Why don't you say something?" She slapped his behind, bit off the umbilical cord, and ran to the crooked door, tearing it open with her left hand, and limped through the divided door out into the autumn gale.

Marie stood on the level windblown field in front of the house, swinging the boy to and fro, while she mumbled a secret formula to Nature's forces. A ragged cloud passed the moon, and the cool light fell upon the landscape and upon the greasy little boy who trembled in the cold. The slight body jerked and very timidly—as if it came from far away—a whimper issued from the baby's lips. He put out his underlip and cried miserably. Marie was content. She walked back to the house, still holding the child by its feet and at arm's length away from herself.

Lars stood petrified and stared at the pot with bubbling water. Marie closed the doors with satisfaction and placed the baby on the table. She rummaged through the kitchen corner and at last found some tattered swaddling clothes and some rags. She dipped a rag in the pot of water, stepped over to the boy, and rubbed him a little. "By Jove, he is not up to much! He is far too frail. You haven't at all gone the full time with him, Johanne. He should have had at least one month more." Marie mulled this over for a while, then she said with authority, "I shall have to baptize him now; I don't think he will live through the night."

"Oh, do you think he should be privately christened?" Johanne sighed. "Couldn't it wait a couple of days? Then my father, the parish clerk at Herlev, will arrive! He can do that. He is coming with Johan."

"No, I wouldn't put it off if I was you," said Marie with great conviction. "He is very delicate, and besides, he is blue all over."

"All right," sighed Johanne from the alcove.

Marie wrapped up the baby and, as traditional practice demanded, she handed him to Lars. For the father should hold the newborn first.

"You are nearest to him; you *are* the father, aren't you?"

"Sure," mumbled Lars. "That stands to reason."

Marie puttered about at the kitchen corner. First she took a pull from the bottle. Then she found a small earthenware bowl on the shelf and poured some water into it from the wooden pail. Then she put the pail next to the fireplace and returned to the table.

Lars kept standing with the newborn baby, looking very shy.

Marie moved to the alcove and picked up the candle, which had burned far down.

"Well then, let us baptize him. What shall he be named?"

Johanne raised herself on one elbow. She was cold under the wet eiderdown, but there was something relieved and sublime about her face. She said in a rather hesitant voice, "Lars and I have talked about it, and if it's a boy, he should be called Peter after my father."

Marie felt comfortable now. That is because she was about to perform the especial and rare deed otherwise entrusted only to clergymen, namely to give the little boy the holy baptism—the sacrament. She straightened her bent figure, looked around, and walked with dignity to the kitchen area, where she emptied the bottle. Then she strutted back to the table and peevishly commanded the dumbfounded Lars, "Hold him over the bowl, you dullard!" While she dipped two arthritic fingers into the bowl and ran them three times over the greasy crown of the newborn baby, she said in an almost clear voice, "Peter, son of Lars Nielsen, I baptize you in the name of the Father and the Son and the Holy Ghost. Amen. Let us say the Lord's Prayer together." Marie looked gratified at Lars and then across to Johanne, who had followed the entire proceedings resting on her elbow.

They said the Lord's Prayer together, and Lars, who had suddenly regained his composure, began to sing "A Mighty Fortress Is Our God."

With his free hand, he took off his cap. When he was finished the singing of the hymn, he handed the baby to Marie. She took the boy with her round to every nook of the room and held the new baby down into every corner, curtsied, and mumbled some secret formulas.

"Well, now it's done as it should be, and you'd better find a fresh candle, Lars Nielsen. Coffee will have to be made, and I have to see if Johanne has delivered the afterbirth. Hurry up! You won't get to bed for the present anyway. And you'll be lucky if that little weakling of a boy makes it through the night."

Two

A few days after the birth came Johanne's father, the parish clerk from Herlev, with Johan. He brought with him different goodies—among other things a little money for Lars Nielsen, who was still without work.

The newborn was unusually small, but he pulled through—contrary to Marie's presumptions.

Sunday the seventh of December in the year 1800 little Peter was presented in Farum church, because Johanne didn't think that the boy should not be in the church at all. Christening Peter at home was not according to her wishes.

The parish clerk Peder Oluf Westergaard from Herlev was also present in the church, and he saw to it that the little family got to the church in style in a horse carriage—and in good time.

Little Peter received a little money as a christening gift, but it was quickly spent on food and firewood as Lars Nielsen went through the whole winter without work.

The seventh of December in the year 1800 was a particularly beautiful December day. Winter had come early, and there was a thin layer of snow everywhere. The sun was shining and made the snow on the tombstones glitter and beam like a mellow dream-coat spread out over an unreal fairy-tale world.

In Farum church everything was bright and friendly, and during the ceremony, Johanne sat with Johan on her lap on the curved bench at the baptismal font. Johan, for his two years, was rather uneasy. Peter—on the contrary—slept se-

cure in the arms of his grandmother, Madam Westergaard.
    Johanne sat and looked at the old sandstone baptismal font with the palm-design and the sanctuary rope. Occasionally, she would move her eyes to the altarpiece and then turn back toward the baptismal font. The altarpiece was divided in four parts. In the two uppermost, the dedication was in Latin; in the two lowermost, in Danish. She had heard that such an altarpiece was called a catechism-piece.
    But she was still so very very tired after the birth, and also worried about the future for her two small boys. Peter was all too small, and Johan coughed too much and often suffered from earaches. She sat and worried about whether the children had enough clothes on—it was now below freezing. Thank heaven for her mother who could sew some things for the children, otherwise Johanne would have had no idea of how to get enough clothes for them to wear. But today the world was bright, because Peter was being presented in church. The sun was shining, and as a result the church did not seem cold at all. The vicar, Henrich Kampmann, stood at the altar and spoke about Jesus' entry into Jerusalem, and peace began to fall on Johanne.
    Lars sat quietly and somewhat bashfully looked at his wooden shoes. Johanne could see that he wasn't paying attention, and she felt a little pang of remorse. Something had disappeared. She no longer had faith in them. They were a family, but she didn't think of them as a family. Lars was no longer the laughing, carefree creature who had strangely broken into her somewhat dull, but secure, life in Herlev.
    She used to walk with Lars on the light-green curved birch twigs straight into the sun. She had not thought about security, money, food, housing, or clothes. She had absorbed and taken his young freckled body to her with pleasure and a bad conscience, since they had neither considered a wedding nor a minister, when she became aware that Johan was coming into the world.

Now she looked down at her red hands that had left off holding onto Johan. All that lay before her were cold nights in the damp alcove and Lars's rough groping hands in her tired lap. Disgust—indifference—where had the sun gone? Oh, if only they could begin again. Why always this desire to start anew? It is always the beginning that is so beautiful.

Johan stood next to the baptismal font and let his small, thin fingers wander in the trimmed palm leaves. She was ready to grab him if he should suddenly decide to run down the church aisle. The congregation joined in singing "A Mighty Fortress Is Our God."

Later, Peter's christening was confirmed, and the congregation spoke its oath and the "Our Father" in unison. They also received a blessing and sang one more hymn.

Johanne sat and thought that she really didn't like Lars's feet. She had always thought that his toes were too fat and fleshy.

Outside the church a light breeze swept over the graves and caused the dream-coat to lighten ever so gently. Like a white cloud it hung momentarily in the air, before drifting down to the graves again as if nothing had happened.

Three

Peter had since moved to Copenhagen and he was living in a house with a gallery, Gammel Mønt 150. He had reached his twenty-seventh year and was unusually short. Yes, he was exactly 163½ centimeters tall. But he was broad and strong, light-haired and blue-eyed. He was healthy and trustworthy in appearance. Everyone liked Peter from Farum.

When he was seventeen years old, he started his apprenticeship as a smith with his uncle in Kalundborg. His father's brother, Christen Nielsen, was a good teacher for him. Peter had waited a long time to become an apprentice as he didn't wish to leave his mother, Johanne. There was his little brother Christian, as well as his sister, Karen Marie, to take his place, but they didn't look after Johanne as well as Peter did.

Johan died, when he was twelve years old. He was buried one humid spring day in the Farum churchyard—a day so rainy and quiet that not a bird dared peep. His parents, along with his mother's father and some neighbors, carried the small coffin to the black hole by the churchyard wall. Peter remembered how the vicar had to shake the spade several times to get the sticky black earth off the blade. The pasty lumps of earth hit the coffin lid down in the hole with a hollow sound. That sound sank deeper and deeper into Peter. It was as if the vicar had hit Johan. They had thrown heavy lumps of dirt on his brother Johan; it pained him inside.

Peter had looked up to Johan, admired him, imitated his

every mannerism, spoken like Johan—even sworn like Johan. They had shared the short wooden bed and slept arm in arm on the flat straw. They had chatted long into the night before falling asleep, and together they had forgotten their hunger. Johan had once given him his bread, even though he himself was hungry. Johan almost never owned anything, but he was always generous. He had dignity—he would never pee while others were present—and he was never coarse. He could swear alright, but he wouldn't listen to the farmhands talk about what they did with the girls when there was a ball. He ran when they began to drivel. Johan always ran and often he got lost in the forest, with Peter following him like a shadow. Whatever Johan thought was good enough for Peter.

Peter was small and broad. Johan was tall and thin. Peter could wear inadequate clothing in the winter and not suffer too much because of it. Johan froze and coughed constantly.

The last time they ran together along Lake Farum was a cold January day. There was ice on the lake and a thin layer of snow over all. Johan wanted to see if the ice was safe. The winter had not been as hard as it usually was, and there hadn't been ice on the lake before now. Johan jumped with his heavy wooden shoes between the rushes, and the ice cracked. One of Johan's wooden shoes disappeared under the ice floe. He had spread himself out on the ice and raked the cold water with both hands to find the shoe, but it was—and remained—gone.

Unhappily Johan had crawled back to the edge of the lake. Peter had watched the whole scene standing on a thick branch overhanging the lake.

Johan sat down in the snow and attempted to pull down the crumpled dirty trousers below his bended knees.

Peter understood it all. Johan had worked an entire year as a herdsboy and had just received the wooden shoes as payment for one year's labor, and now one of them was gone.

It was so hard to bear. Johan's toes became blue from the cold. The brothers limped their way home to the crooked house. Peter supported Johan as well as he could while they limped along. Nevertheless, Johan had to put his bare foot down in the snow once in a while.

When they got home, their father was already home from work. For once he had been able to find something to do at one of the farms, and as usual had been to the grocer for a bottle of schnapps.

The slightly lazy Lars was suddenly furious about the loss of the wooden shoe. He beat Johan until Johanne came between them. She pulled Lars away from the boy. Johan cried and moaned from sheer excitement and, on top of this, had begun to cough.

Suddenly the worst happened. Johan coughed up blood—lots of blood. Peter felt as if the room was gone. In spite of his mere eleven years, he realized what this meant—Johan would die.

Lars became very unhappy and drank so much schnapps that he had to lie down in the alcove.

Johanne put the shaking Johan to bed, and she ordered Peter to lie down beside him to keep Johan warm. They had no firewood in the house.

Peter did not leave Johan's side the rest of the night and slept hardly at all.

The next day Johan did not need Peter's warmth, as he had gotten a high fever.

Johan lived almost two months, until March. Peter slept next to him during his whole period of illness. During the day, Peter tried to earn a pair of wooden shoes as a herdsboy at the neighbor's farm. But as soon as he had an idle moment, he ran home to Johan.

He became thinner and thinner, and his eyes bigger and bigger. Sometimes he tried to get out of bed, but he always became dizzy and had to lie down again. Occasionally he and Peter could talk together about their neighbor Mads Petersen's fine buggy, and about how the wagon could be improved by adjusting the wheels.

Even though Peter was dead tired when he came home at night, he looked at Johan and tried to anticipate his every wish. Johan was almost always thirsty because of the fever, and Peter ran for the water ladle. He wanted desperately to give Johan milk or juice, but they had none in the house. Only once did the doctor come. It was his grandmother who had arranged it. The doctor had simply shaken his head and said "Consumption, nothing can be done." Under his breath he added: "These people should never have had children. They are not in a position to take reasonable care of them."

One morning the thin, light boy with the big blue eyes lay still and completely stiff. Peter woke early; he could sense that Johan's body no longer radiated warmth.

He sat up in the bed. Johan's eyes were still blue but they were no longer shining. They were only fuzzy and dismal. Peter slipped over to the alcove. In the weak early morning light he touched cautiously his mother's one arm, lying thin and frozen on top of the quilt. Johanne looked first at Peter and then at the bed in corner. Neither of them spoke.

The rainy day when Johan was buried in the Farum churchyard touched something inside of Peter. He became generous. Nothing was to be forgotten, not even services, and everything in the world should be used for the enjoyment of others. Peter became just as helpful as Johan had been. And he left his mother's side only reluctantly. He followed her like a shadow. Johanne never spoke of Johan, and neither did Peter. But it was as if the fair boy was with them like a shadow in the room. The boy had been as mild as the sun's gentle fingers, when they played in the summertime waters of Lake Farum.

Four

Peter sighed and stopped. Strange thing about the past—it never lets you go. Past, present, what does it really mean to be a human being? It is not everything that is remembered. Sometimes things get distorted in the memory. Maybe it didn't really happen that way. We think there is a truth, but it is colored by what we want to remember or, deepest down, by what we desire. Can one take anything at all seriously when one dare not trust oneself and one's own thoughts?

Peter had hoped that one day he could come forward as a whole human being, complete and perfect. But he was, however, never finished with the past, and a part of him was working on the future and all those plans he had always had. Why could he never be here and now as a man?

Why was he always running away? He felt like someone who couldn't fill out the moment, one who could never find his inner self. The present—life—was never there.

He went over to a window in the gallery and looked down at the narrow backyard. It was drizzling. The cobblestones in the yard were shiny and soft from the rain.

He longed to get away—away from the narrow backyard and gallery. There must be something more one place or another outside Copenhagen. Life must exist one place or another. He was twenty-seven years old now. Young but, nevertheless, not really that young.

He has worked hard as a blacksmith's apprentice under different masters. Two years ago he had become a master blacksmith. Now he wanted to have a trade license!

Until recently he had wanted this passionately. He had been a man with initiative, a young man who wanted to become a blacksmith and have a license to trade in Copenhagen.

She married someone else. Her father, the blacksmith Sigersted, held the wedding, and he—Peter from Farum—was invited as a dear friend of the family and because he worked in the forge. For several years he had loved her. He had worked for her father in the forge, and he had watched her every day; he felt her nearness. He had taken it for granted that they would get married someday. Imagine, he had been that simpleminded. Last Christmas he had even kissed her. She pretended it was just for fun. That should have brought him back to reality. He was a short man; she was tall and slender. And he had kissed her while she sat down. He leaned his forehead against the window. Oh, it was a curse to be short.

When he ate Sunday dinner with the blacksmith, he had held her hand secretly. She had always smiled and acted friendly, but now it was obvious that something had been missing. He had overlooked the most important thing: The fact that she was not in love with him at all. He was a ridiculous little man without a sense of reality. He realized that now. This dark slender girl with the brown curls tied on her head with a silk ribbon. He had looked into her brown eyes and hoped for one single small promise, but he had never felt really sure. He had felt, though, that they belonged together. Every time he left from the Sunday dinner, he felt lonely and sad. He looked forward so much to these dinners—and what came of it all?

In the spring, when he had been ill with fever in his room, he had dreamt and hoped that she would come and stand there in the room with a jug of soup for him. But she never came. She just smiled when they passed each other in the forge or in the yard—she always smiled.

He asked no one in particular, "Regitze, if I had been

as tall as your father, would you have seen me and felt that I was a real man?" How often had he, in his thoughts, asked her this: "If I had been as tall as other men—would you then?"

He looked out at the rain, and imagined being one with the moist air, to be a raindrop bursting against a damp cobblestone and then disappearing into the ground between the slippery stones.

When he saw them together at the engagement, he went home to his room quickly. There he sat at his pinewood table—powerless and silent. He no longer knew himself. He felt like roaring uncontrollably without considering whether anyone could hear him. A little later he was crying, and he hit the table with his big blacksmith fists. He just hit the table, completely aimless and powerless. He tried to explain to himself that he was foolish. He was demanding love from this creature selected by his ego—his hunger. The girl was all right; she just didn't love him. Not him, but someone else. A nice-looking young man from a good family with a good background. She had never considered the short crooked-legged blacksmith from Farum as a regular admirer.

I'm the reason myself, he thought. *I needed that dream to brighten up the many gray days. I needed something to get up for every day. Something to get washed for. I would have never used my clean shirts if it hadn't been for her.* Even though he didn't see her every day, the possibility was there. Because of her, he had the strength to get his tired legs out of bed on the many dark and ice-cold winter mornings. He needed this infatuation. This wonderful thing on the horizon. But now what? There was no longer any reason to continue. He would have to get his own workshop. A life without her—the world was different now. Where should he go from here?

He was surprised over his grief. How should he get rid of his grief? Behind the grief was just a big black hole of indifference. Regitze! Why had she been so indifferent? Why so obliging and friendly and yet so indifferent? He understood that he had never owned just a small space in her life. He had never owned even one small corner of her consciousness.

He suddenly felt insecure around other people. He felt he was becoming afraid of people. He had felt it yesterday when he was together with the other blacksmiths. He was uncertain and withdrawn. He no longer believed in their kindness, and at the same time he felt an urge to please them.

Why could he no longer behave naturally with them? What was it they had talked about yesterday when they were sitting drinking in the small inn at Graabrødre Square? Oh yes, it was still in his subconscious mind—America!

Five

Peter turned away from the window and walked from the gallery into the small living room and over to the table. There was a letter on the table. It was his petition to be deleted from the recruitment roll and transferred to Copenhagen's civil militia. This was necessary if he wanted to receive a license in Copenhagen; then he could finally establish himself as a master smith in the city. He wanted so much to become a master smith, to be his own man without having to work for others. The letter on the table cost him a lot to have written.
   He read:

The 21st of March 1827.
   Peter Larsen Farum, blacksmith apprentice and soldier of the Reserve Battalion 1st Life Guards Regiment, registered conscript No. 3181 entered on the Recruitment Roll in the District of Copenhagen, does most humbly petition to be deleted from the aforementioned Recruitment Roll and transferred to Copenhagen's Civil Militia in order to become eligible for a License to Trade as Master Smith in this city.

Most humbly drafted by
C. Dencher,
Copyist, residing at No. 184 Holmensgade
1st Floor.

Peter walked over to his wall cabinet and found writing tools and paper. He had to go on with this matter. He refused to think about Regitze. He would only think about his future. He would show her that he could make it. Sometimes he felt all too acutely that when Regitze had her husband and children to care for, she would not care at all about the little smith from Farum.

He walked back to the table and put down the ink bottle and the writing tools. He pulled out the chair and sat down with determination. With his rough smith hands he smoothed out the paper. It was difficult for him to write. He had practiced a lot, and he felt that his handwriting had improved. They would not be able to say about him, the smith from Farum, that he could not write in a proper way.

He started:

To the King.

I, the undersigned—born in Farum in the district of Copenhagen, registered conscript No. 3181 on this year's Recruitment Roll, having resided from early youth in Kalundborg where I learned from my father's brother the trade of smith, in which trade I took my apprentice's papers in 1823, and since that time having lawfully resided in Copenhagen where I have had employment with master smiths in the city, and for the two years past as master journeyman for Master Blacksmith Sigersted, in whose service I have shown skill at my trade and have conducted myself well at all times, witness my master's letter of recommendation enclosed herewith—being now in my twenty-seventh year, have mind to establish myself as Master Blacksmith and Licensed Trader in this city but am hindered herein, being a conscript and therefore unable to obtain a License to Trade.

Although I have been passed over in the recruitment of troops of the line, partly by reason of my insufficient height and also by reason of the drawing of lots, I have now because of my age been posted to the Reserve Battalions, witness the copy of my enrollment papers herewith enclosed, namely 1st Life Guards Regiment 3rd Battalion. Being unskilled in the use of arms, I will be put to the Copenhagen Garrison Drill School, thus being forced to leave my present employment, and you must see my pleasant prospects for the future come to naught.

Through the Grace of Your Majesty, others in my position have been granted permission to transfer to the Civil Militia, and having learned a useful and advantageous trade with which I could obtain a License to Trade and establish myself as Master Tradesman in this city and as my entire earthly happiness rests on my release from fulfilling my conscription in the usual way and coming under the Reserve Battalion as I have already written, I make bold to hope for Your Majesty's sympathetic ear as I most humbly petition for Your Majesty's most gracious ordinance to grant removal of my name from the Recruitment Roll and release me from conscription, on the condition that I join Copenhagen's Defence Militia forthwith and that I procure the regulation uniform.

Most humbly,
Peter Lassen, Farum

  Peter had worked hard on the letter, and he felt very tired now. It was always the signature that was the most difficult. Because his real name was Peter Nielsen. But when he was a child in Farum and Herlev and later on in Kalundborg, he was always called Peter, Lars's son from Farum. Therefore he began calling himself Larsen, and sometimes he signed his name as Lassen. He liked the name Lassen best.

  He got up, walked over to the cabinet again, and found a new piece of paper. It was a recommendation from his master Sigersted—Regitze's father. Thoughtfully he weighed it in his hand.

He remembered very clearly when Sigersted wrote it. It was a Sunday evening. Regitze looked so beautiful in a blue dress. She helped the maid carry in and out the food from the table. She had seemed so soft and helpful. Whenever she would pass his chair with something in her hands, it happened that she would touch his neck with the back of her hand. Was this really accidentally and without meaning? To Peter, it had meant happiness so great that he could not sleep at night. He was lying there thinking about the soft brush of her hands.

After dinner, he and the master smith sat in the small living room smoking. Peter had asked him about the letter of recommendation, and Sigersted had written it while they sat there in the room. Peter had felt so happy—mainly because she was close—and in his thoughts he had pretended that he was Sigersted's son-in-law.

He looked down at the paper he had in his hand.

> Journeyman Smith Peter Larsen, Farum, has had employment with me as Master Journeyman for the last two years, being a most able worker at his trade and having always conducted himself most well.
>
> Witness by my hand, Copenhagen 15th Day of March 1827.
> P. Sigersted
> Master Blacksmith
> Residing at No. 335 Dronningens Tvergade

Peter carefully put the three papers on top of each other. He had to get them mailed in the morning.

He could not handle any more Sunday dinners together with Regitze and her husband.

He walked out on the gallery. It was getting dark now. It was still raining. Spring was on its way; in a couple of days it would be April.

The rain fell steadily on the cobblestones down in the

narrow yard. Everything seemed so quiet. The moisture and the darkness filled the gallery.

He was thinking that he would probably never experience what other men take for granted. *Was it the chance of your life passing by?* he asked himself. He did not want any more fantasies about Regitze. Oh, how he had dreamt about her and about her body. He had wallowed in her in his fantasies. Now there was only the darkness and the rain left, and with it a strange serene sadness. He saw the contour of himself in the windows of the gallery. Would she perhaps have loved him if he had been a tall man? Should he perhaps have proposed a long time ago, before the young man came into the picture? Peter meant to wait until he had made master smith with his own workshop. Then he would have had something to offer her.

His thoughts circled around without means like dry stones rolling on the beach.

His father had just died in Hillerød! Peter did not go to the funeral. He hoped that Karen Marie and Christian, his sister and brother, had been there. Peter had a bad conscience. He should have gone to Hillerød. He could have gotten a ride up there. He felt bad toward Johanne, not having gone.

Oh, it was like Regitze had broken everything. Before, he would have done anything for his mother, but he dared not even leave Copenhagen for a few days to go to the funeral. Imagine if Regitze during just those days wanted to see him, maybe give him a message! Imagine if she felt like taking a walk with him! The most wonderful things could have happened. Now that she was married, the dreams would have to stop.

His old worn-out and drunken father only lived to fifty. His face had always seemed old. His tired, sour father, without happiness, without life, had always been old. Peter could not feel any sorrow because his father was dead. He never felt secure and happy with him. Now Peter felt strangely sad about the life his father had lived—that poor life without happiness.

Aggression and anger filled Peter at the thought. This wasted life filled him with sadness.

Another thought turned up and crowded his mind —*America!* There everyone could find work. In America the real life could be lived.

him in Copenhagen, or in Denmark for that matter. He did not want to stay any longer in places where he had suffered defeats. He did not want to think about hunger and poverty anymore. He did not want to be remembered as the one who was running barefoot in the fields in Farum. He did not want to think about all the hard and dirty labour in Kalundborg or at the different blacksmiths in Copenhagen. He did not want to think about a girl with long black eyelashes and a wonderful body that he would not ever be able to hold. No, it had to end now! There had to be something else. He could not face a new winter with more lonesome walks in Copenhagen and more visits to inns. Now the goal was America!

Holst had toasted him and said, "Hey, you there, you should try something new. If you never try anything, nothing ever happens." Holst had promised to help Peter to get his passport and papers in order, because then they could go together to Boston.

Peter had gone home to Gammel Mønt 150 to sleep in order to get sober. After that he had locked himself in with the ink bottle and feather pen. Now he had to work, and fast.

He wrote carefully and neatly:

Copenhagen the 17th of September 1830
    Peter Lassen, Farum, Master Blacksmith, Civil Artilleryman No. 126, 4th Company, most humbly requests gracious permission to travel to the new Danish colony in America notwithstanding his having served as conscript registered as No. 3181 on the Recruitment Roll in the District of Copenhagen, as he cannot make a livelihood in this city.
                  Most humbly,
                  Peter Lassen, Farum
                  written by the supplicant himself

Peter packed his things and let Holst and the apprentice Olsen check the luggage.

He also sold some of his tools to Sigersted, who gave him a good price because of their old friendship. Now Peter had enough money for the ticket, but that was about it.

Now there was only one thing left, and that was Johanne! He had to see his mother, who now lived in Hillerød. He had to find Johanne and say good-bye to her in a nice way.

Peter got a lift to Hillerød and found his mother in a side wing of a large farmhouse. Here she was supporting herself by helping in the kitchen.

She had two small rooms and a small kitchen to herself.

The year before Peter had exchanged a few letters with the surrogate court and with Johanne's two brothers, because Peter had to persuade them to give up their inheritance from their father, the schoolmaster in Herlev, who finally died a very old man. Peter had emphasized that Johanne was very poor.

The two brothers were both wealthy farmers, and neither of them needed more bread on the table. The brothers had agreed to let Johanne inherit their shares.

Now she was trying to hold onto the money. Therefore, she had kept her job at the farm. Peter suspected her, however, of giving some of the money to her youngest son, Christian, who, like his father, was always out of work.

And there Peter was, sitting in Johanne's simple room in Hillerød. There was not much furniture in the room, an alcove—a table with some chairs around it and a small bench by the wall. The household goods had not expanded. The three English faience plates were a wedding gift for Karen Marie. But the clock hanging on the wall was counting time with loud ticks. One new thing had been added, however, a chair with a high back and upholstery. Johanne had inherited it from her father.

Now she was sitting in it and thoughtfully watching Peter sitting opposite her at the small table.

"So you want to go to America, Peter?" she said quietly. Peter looked at his mother. *How old is she now? Somewhere in her fifties?* She looked old. Her hair was grayish yellow and tied in a simple knot in the back. Her black dress was worn and the apron was dirty. The worst part for him was to see her hands bent from arthritis. They looked red and worn.

"Yes Mother, there is no future for a blacksmith in Copenhagen. I want to work and use my strength, but nobody needs me. Nobody needs my strength. Even though I'm small, I am a strong man."

Johanne nodded her head. "Yes, you are strong. Yes, but if you can find work over there in the new country I guess it will be alright. Isn't it dangerous with all that new? What kind of a country is it, America?"

Peter didn't quite know where to end or where to begin speaking about America. He had heard so much about this country, but one never knows until one has seen it with one's own eyes.

"It is a big country. There are mountains and forests and there's enough land for everybody. People from all over Europe are going there. In the south it is warm all year round and in the north it is very cold. I have heard they have snow on the mountains. They speak the English language over there. There are also some places in the south where they speak French. I don't know any of these languages, so it doesn't matter for me." Peter smiles, and a little color has come to his cheeks.

Johanne looked as if she wanted something, but she didn't really have the power. Instead she said quietly, "I guess I won't see you anymore then." In her tired face there came a painful look. "Have you got all the money you need? Or . . ." She was pointing with a crooked finger towards the wall cabinet. "I have a little bit left of the inheritance."

Peter shook his head. No, he could not take anything from Johanne. He would rather starve. He remembered in a distant cloud the cold winters and Johan, freezing his bare feet in the winter cold. As an echo of loneliness he remembered the cold walks in the churchyard of Farum, the hunger, Lars's screaming and drunken talk, the ice on Lake Farum, and a blond smiling boy. A distant picture slid by, a picture of Johan's hands—the blue swollen hands—lying on the cover that morning when he found his brother dead next to himself in the bed.

He looked at Johanne's face; it looked like a country—a country that is dried out and has put its stony earth on top of all life and movements. "Mother," he whispered, "I want to live. I have a right to live." While he was saying this, Regitze's smile penetrated him like the serrated blunt knife of hopelessness.

Johanne got up, rocked from the chair over to the wall, and took the clock down. She pressed the box of the clock against her flat chest, and the ticks of the clock disappeared in her dirty apron. "You are going to have this clock, because you were always the best."

Peter got up and reluctantly accepted Johanne's only treasure. She looked around for more. With dragging feet, she walked over to the small window. The small square windows were covered with vapor as they looked over the farmer's garden.

In the crooked windowsill stood a clay mug with an old pipe. The pipe bowl was made of porcelain and had a small picture of a deer painted on it. The deer was standing quietly in front of two pine trees. The pipe handle was intact.

"I want you to have your father's pipe, too. You took such good care of me when he died."

Peter accepted the pipe. They stood for a little while in the quiet room. The gray fall light was shining through the small windows, and Peter felt his loneliness to the fullest. He knew that when he left Hillerød tomorrow, he would leave the only person who ever really knew him. Wherever he would go in the world he would only meet strangers. They would experience him only as they saw him, as he appeared. They would never know who he really was and how he became the person he was. But in Hillerød in Denmark in a small gray room there sat a quiet and unhappy woman who knew his soul. She would be without family when he came to America. No one would know anything about the ice on Lake Farum or how the church bell sounded when it announced the sunset on the long light summer evenings in Farum. No one would know anything about a blond smiling boy called Johan, whom Peter used to share his bed with and gave warmth to as his life ran out.

Johanne was his last link to the past.

Seven

The next day Peter left Hillerød. Johanne did not say much. She did not follow him to the crossroad where the mail wagon was supposed to pick him up. The stony landscape had closed itself over her face. There was no more to say.

She watched him walk through the driveway. Then she hurried back to the kitchen and scullery to bake rye bread.

Peter went back to Copenhagen. In a way, he would have liked to say good-bye to Christian and Karen Marie. But Johanne was not sure where Christian was at the moment, and Karen Marie lived too far away. His only comfort was that he could write them from America.

When he came back to his lodgings in Gammel Mønt, difficulties were waiting for him. Holst had been there and left a message saying that Peter could not get his passport unless he was granted dismissal from the civil artillery corps. This permission he would have to have as soon as possible to be ready for the departure of the ship in late September. Peter immediately took out the ink bottle and paper from his wall cabinet and wrote the following:

To the King,
    At your Majesty's almighty resolution of the fourth of April 1827, it was bestowed on me in the district of Copenhagen as a registered conscript No. 3181 on this year's Recruitment Roll, to serve the time I otherwise had to serve at the Reserve Battalions at the Civil Artillery Corps, and I became thereafter on the tenth of

May of the same year employed at said Civil Artillery Corps fourth company No. 126, at which position I dare believe I have fulfilled my duties. On the twenty-fifth of August 1827 I achieved my trade license as a blacksmith here in the city, but experience has unfortunately convinced me that I cannot find livelihood here, as in spite of all diligence and thrift, I have declined in such a way that I am in no way able to live here, and destitution has forced me to the decision of letting myself enroll in the newly established colony in America where my clothes have already been sent, as I in my ignorance believed that nothing would hinder my dismissal from the corps.

As I, however, experience the opposite—namely the military service incumbent on me from which I cannot resign without higher resolution, my true happiness must depend upon my departure from this city, so that I will not only become a burden to the welfare system. I dare most humbly to emplore Your Majesty by your almighty resolution to allow my resignation from the Civil Artillery Corps and my departure for America, in the hope of settling there.

    Most humbly,
    Peter Lassen, Farum
    Blacksmith and civil artilleryman
    residing at Gammel Mønt 150, 1st sidefloor

  A few days later Peter got his permission to leave the corps. He didn't make the ship leaving in late September. The carpenter, Holst, and the apprentice, Olsen, were very keen on them all going to America together. Therefore they waited on for the next ship, which was supposed to leave from Elsinore on October 12th. It was going by way of London with freight, and here it would also load other goods for Boston. Peter and his travel companions traveled with the mail wagon to Elsinore. The luggage was sent ahead and brought on board.

A cool fall rain fell on the cobblestones in Elsinore's streets, as they drove through the town toward the habor.

Peter was quiet. His two travel companions were somewhat giddy and in high spirits at their coming departure. They had said good-bye to their relatives in Copenhagen, and because the departure had been a little delayed, they had made several last-minute visits.

Peter had said good-bye to Sigersted and his wife, but he had not visited Regitze in her new home. He had thought about it, but his courage failed. His flagging self-confidence didn't allow it. No, no more humiliations. It was over. Peter had been sitting looking at the fall forest during the trip—the wet Danish fall forest, which he would never see again.

Now he was thinking about Johanne. How long would she be able to make it on the small inheritance from her father, the schoolmaster? If he became rich in America he could send her some money. Karen Marie and Christian could take care of her. But they didn't have very much either. Christian was out of work for the time being, and Karen Marie's husband drank too much.

Peter was listening to the sound of the horses' hooves against the cobblestones. They changed horses on the way. Now they made quickly for the harbor.

He would never see Johanne again. He was going into something that he could not foresee at all. He wished it would never rain in America. Rain made him lonely and reminded him that he was a very poor man now. All he owned he invested in the ticket. But he would work, he would become something—he was going to live!

On the twelfth of October in the year 1830, a short light-haired man walked on board the *Sankt Marie* in Elsinore. His big mouth was firmly closed and his blue eyes had a strange expression of clearness and sorrow.

Eight

It's a long way from Boston to California!
It had taken him ten years to get there. The emigrant ship went alongside the quay in Boston in February in the year 1831.
It was easy for a clever blacksmith to get work in Boston, but after a few months he had to move on. He no longer needed a fixed address. To tie yourself down to places, houses, and people was not that important anymore.
The world was big and exciting, yes, almost overwhelming for one single man. The boredom, though, was the worst. To grow into the habit of a permanent job, so necessary for achieving freedom—the real life—was not for Peter. When work had become something that just had to be done, then it was no longer a job, but slavery. The worst, he knew, was that he was just accepted as a piece of inventory in a workshop or in a house. When they yawned and said to themselves, "Oh, there is the blacksmith Peter Lassen from Denmark," then it was time to change place.
He had felt the bitter pain of rejection in his mind; this tear in his soul, which hurt in the palms of his hands; this pain, which always returned. No, he did not want to just be accepted! He didn't want to be the one who made somebody yawn. Peter had learned that his home was where he himself found a reason for being.
He had nobody to consider. He had no wife or children waiting for him anywhere. He was a free man who could leave when he made his surroundings yawn.

Behind the painful palms of his hands there was a small, unattainable light on the horizon, distant and flickering—Regitze.

Ten years is a long time to be traveling. The sun bleaches your hair, and it starts to turn gray.

The first time in Boston had been difficult, because Peter didn't know the language. How incompetent he had felt when he couldn't explain what he meant!

He had been sitting there like a mute between the workers in the evening, drinking with them. They had barely noticed his existence. He couldn't answer them, and they always became angry when he interrupted them and, stuttering, tried to explain something.

But he was a quick learner. Every day he got something from them. He would learn the names of this and that. He did not want to be a defenseless prey for the fickle wind.

When he first started to understand them, there was one word that they kept repeating. It was the word *west*. It dawned on him that all immigrants with respect for themselves traveled on toward the west.

Incidentally, Boston was not the America he had dreamt about. The whole thing reminded him too much of Copenhagen. Of course the streets were much wider, and there were more horse carriages, but the whole atmosphere was wrong.

He worked day and night and listened to the workers at the inn. "Go west!"

When he had saved enough money, he traveled as far as the money went, that being Keytesville in Chariton country. Here they needed a blacksmith. Peter bought land and became rich.

It took time, how long is difficult to say. Time can never be measured. Far out on the horizon, time is casting its long pale sunbeams over the mountains—the mountains with the creaking dry earth and loose stones. Time is like a lazy wave in the river or like the blackbirds singing in the twilight at Lake Farum, until the bird finally finds a tree or a hedge for the night. Where did time go? Impossible to say, as with the small birds in the twilight. Time changes with the light. Not to be reached, like slumbering birch branches in the Nordic summer night.

Keytesville was a town for men. Peter preferred relaxing with men. Women made him uneasy and longing. He only wanted to be together with men. Therefore—and to protect himself against the women—he applied for membership with the Masonic Order in Warren Lodge No. 74, Keytesville. This Order brought him many happy hours.

They could not handle the Indians in Keytesville. The Sioux Indians were too wild. The people in the city had a difficult time organizing themselves against them. But Peter had served in the civic guards of Copenhagen. In the year 1838 he established a new civic guard corps. The little broad man from Denmark was getting respect in the city. He taught the citizens of Keytesville something new. He taught them how to kill Indians.

It's not that he liked to kill them. The first time he shot an Indian it felt like when he was a child and his cat had sunk its claws in a blackbird. The cat threw the bleeding bird in front of his feet. He felt pity for the bird. He knew that it couldn't live and the best he could do was to kill it. He bent down and picked up the bird from the yard. Carefully he took it with both hands. He held the little warm body in his hands for a short while. Then he closed his eyes and threw it with all his force against the edge of the doorstep. He felt sick. When he opened his eyes he saw that the blow had not killed the bird. It was lying with the wings spread out on the doorstep, panting. One of the eyes was damaged and the beak was halfway open.

He bent down in horror, picked it up again, and hit it against the doorstep, again and again, until the bird's head hung slack down on the side. He threw it down and ran over to the pump. His hands were red from the blood.

That's the way he felt about the Indians. Most of the men in the town were proud every time they killed a savage, but Peter just felt that he had performed a dirty job.

The savages had attacked women and children from the town. That's why the Indians had to be exterminated. It was one thing to steal cattle, but to kill children was unforgivable. Peter felt that it was his duty to intervene.

The people in Keytesville could not recognize the Indians as equals. They said that the Indians were savage, animal-like, and cruel.

Peter felt that the Indians were angry at the white people. In the beginning he did not know why. Many years had to pass before Peter really understood their anger.

The first time he killed one of them, he felt like a murderer. He didn't talk about it. The dying Indian was lying on the ground at his feet, writhing in pain. He sent Peter a look so full of hatred, and he used his last strength to grasp for the knife in his belt. Peter was shocked with himself. He had felt that it was his duty to help the town with the Indian problem, now he felt only guilt; there had to be another way to solve this problem. This strong man lying on the ground, rolling in agony in his leather loincloth, carried so many proud feathers around his forehead that he terrified Peter. He had made Peter a murderer. The Indian's eyes slowly turned big and humble. He achieved that surprised and powerless expression that Peter knew so well. He had so often seen this warm expression in the eyes of animals bleeding to death. The proud man submitted himself to the heavy weather, the droughts, and the endless loneliness. He saw something distant.

Peter never spoke about how many he killed in the town's Indian battles, but he tried hard to hit the target when he shot. And Peter had many thoughts about the Indians. From his time in the civic guards of Copenhagen, Peter was brought up to defend the city and to realize that it was sometimes necessary to kill.

He had never anticipated, though, that he would one day really have to kill another human being. He felt guilt. He aimed at them when they came galloping. They were always inside a dust cloud. They were painted all over, and they were screaming and hooting. He couldn't help being afraid of them.

It was so easy to shoot; pull the trigger and the man fell off the horse—dead.

When he was hidden securely, he could fire away at them. He was the master of life and death. Of course they wanted to kill him too, if they could. He knew that, but the Indians were only a few, and someday they would all be gone—exterminated. It was not a worthy fight. He got thoughts like that every now and then, especially in the evening when he was sitting in his nice log cabin working with some tool in front of the fireplace.

It was always an impossible responsibility to take the life of another human being. These bodies, how dead they were. The savage Indian suddenly became small and silent. Where was everything else? Where was the man? Left on the ground was the shell of a body. But the strength—where was that? Where were the screams, the power, and the will to fight and survive?

Peter looked at death differently after the battles with the Indians in Keytesville. Life was no longer for everybody, but for those who took it in their own hands. Death was a reality that could hit anyone who didn't take care. Death hit indiscriminately. It wasn't always the brave and the wise who survived, but the lucky and the fast.

This outlook on life and death, the disgust he felt at shooting Indians, made it difficult for him to sustain his belief in God. After he had come to America, he could no longer find God.

The Indians' attacks on Keytesville weakened when rumors spread among the tribes that the small blond giant had taken command in the town. Everybody respected the small "captain."

And then John A. Sutter came to Keytesville.

Nine

"We are going to California," said Sutter. "I'm on my way. You can come later. Get some people together and come to California. You can stay with me."

Sutter was always incredibly hospitable and generous, and he completely overlooked the fact that he owned neither house nor land. He invited everybody to stay with him once they came to California.

"California is fertility itself. The weather in California is mild. The Indians will eat out of your hands. There is lots of gold and metals. What in the world are you doing in this hole of Keytesville?!"

Peter Lassen was convinced. Not because Sutter inspired confidence, but because he had heard the same enthusiastic words from others who were passing through. Everybody seemed to agree that California was something special.

Sutter had made an impression on Peter. The man was elegant and courteous and he behaved with a dignity and authority far above the small Dane's. Sutter was tall, narrow-faced, his eyes were both determined and a little dreamy, and his moustache was well trimmed.

Sutter left Keytesville in a hurry, and Peter promised together with some of the others from town to follow.

Sutter had said very naturally that all they had to do was to ask for "Sutter's Fort" when they arrived in California. Because it was there that everything in the future was going to happen. It was from there that all the affairs of California would be directed.

When Peter finally reached the coast of California, ten years had passed since he left Boston.

The journey through the prairie had been long and hard. Finally he reached the coast, and he and his travel companions sailed down it. The name of the ship was *Lausanne*, and they had had trouble with the Mexicans in getting permission to go ashore at Bodega. But the Russians from Fort Ross had protected them, and got them ashore in one piece. From here they started on their long wanderings!

This was the country where they were going to build. *Everything is possible here*, Peter thought. The question was, however, where should he start. Peter settled down in Santa Cruz and built California's first sawmill. The mill became a success, and Peter prospered and bought cattle.

Should he found a town here? No, something was missing. It wasn't the right place. The place where his town would be had to be completely different. It had to be fertile and with a good connection to the surrounding areas by means of a main river. The place also had to be center for travelers, the people coming from the east as well as the people going west to the coast. When Peter had become known and appreciated in the Santa Cruz area, he sold his sawmill to Isaac Graham.

The people in Santa Cruz were sad because they liked the little helpful Dane so much. He had done so much for them and often asked so little in return. Now he disappeared again, and no one knew where to.

Peter bought one hundred head of cattle with the money and then he went to Sacramento through San José.

The cattle followed him and his anvil. What is a blacksmith without an anvil?

When Peter hit the anvil, the cattle came.

One day he reached Sutter's Fort.

Peter was very impressed. He was no ordinary man, this Sutter. What a fort he had built! The fort was surrounded by a wall six meters tall and one meter wide. He had even gotten hold of some old ship cannons. Behind the wall there were all kinds of different workshops, and some very well disciplined Indians took turns standing guard. Sutter wanted to be addressed as "captain." Yes, he had become a great man in California.

When the rumor spread that Peter had arrived with at least one hundred head of cattle, Sutter told one of his Indians to show Peter into his office. Sutter found it appropriate to meet Peter halfway.

"Greetings, noble friend," Sutter said with great dignity and an overwhelming arm movement. "I knew you would come. Everybody finds their way to Sutter's Fort. Everybody with any brains, I might add. You will stay, naturally. I need a good blacksmith."

Peter smiled a little evasively and sat down on a crooked unsteady chair by the desk right across from Sutter. "Maybe," he said. He dreamt about starting something himself—a town.

"You will come and have dinner with me tonight? I always have at least twenty guests for dinner. You can just let the Indians look after your cattle."

Peter looked around searchingly. "You need some furniture. Furniture you don't have to be ashamed of, anyway. If you give me lodgings and look after my cattle, I will make you some good furniture."

Sutter nodded his head, apparently preoccupied. Actually, he was thrilled at the thought of getting consistent furniture, but you should never be too obvious.

Peter made furniture for Sutter as well as for some of the others. Many were wondering why he slept so little. Peter was always the first who got up in the morning and the last one to go to bed at night.

He also made wagon wheels and very quickly became the town's jack-of-all-trades. Naturally, Sutter found it quite reasonable that Peter did his best to keep the fort going.

But Peter was doing more than Sutter knew about. Secretly he was selling the hides brought in by the people of the hunting expedition. He bought cattle with the money. His herd was growing and growing.

Behind the walls of Sutter's Fort was an area 166 meters long and 50 meters wide. It was easy to oversee what was going on, which people came and went.

Peter was following everything closely. That's why it was a complete surprise to him when some white immigrants succeeded in stealing a horse and a mule from him. He became very angry. How dare they steal his animals! The total value was approximately seventy-five dollars, and that represented a lot of money.

It was John Bidwell's job to supervise the men guarding the cattle, and Peter told him that it was his duty to reimburse the stolen livestock. "It is after all you who have been told by Sutter to look after my property."

Peter could feel that John Bidwell was not anxious to reimburse anything.

Therefore Peter suggested something else. "We could go together and pursue the thieves."

This proposition suited John much better, and he got hold of a third man for the journey, a German by the name of James Bruheim.

There was no map of the area to which they were going. None of the local places had been named yet. Therefore Peter drew up a map, step by step, as the small party forced their way through the terrain. He felt responsibility toward the people who would someday follow the same route. It could mean death for the travelers if he made a mistake.

Peter and his travel companions competed in finding good names for the different places. The first night they camped by a hilltop, a butte, and the river running by they named Butte Creek.

But they didn't see the horse thieves. It took days before

they found the trail and things got moving. The more they caught up with the thieves, the more excited Peter got. It wasn't because of the horse and the mule; he could easily do without them. What comes easy goes just as easy. No, it was the sport of it! The challenge of hunting these men.

Peter was also excited over this lovely country here, so fertile, so full of wildlife—his town should be founded around here. All possibilities were at hand here.

They came to a new river, which they called Deer Creek because of the caribou and the big red stags. Here by Deer Creek he would found his town. When he came back to Sutter's Fort, he would immediately ask permission to acquire all this land.

At the bank of the Sacramento, the trail of the horse thieves ended. John sat on his horse and could see people on the opposite bank. "Look, there are some people over there and they are white. It's them, the bastards," he yelled excitedly.

The German answered, "The current is too strong here. I don't think we can get across."

James Bruheim was getting tired from this breathless riding through the wilderness. He didn't feel safe about the Indians. Peter kept explaining to him that when he, Peter Lassen, was there, nothing would happen. Peter always made great efforts with these people. It had become an obsession with him to make friends with every Indian he met in the wilderness. It was easier than shooting them. James never took any chances concerning the savages. He simply didn't trust them.

Peter had already dismounted and had begun cutting down trees. James sighed. That man simply wore him out. He could see that Peter was making a raft. Imagine such great effort for a couple of poor hacks.

Well, the end would probably be that he would get his animals back.

During the day Peter and John built a raft, and then they went out into the current. Peter had done his work well but everything almost went wrong anyway. They landed two miles further down the river than they had anticipated. They were wet and exhausted, and the German wanted to just lie down. But John and Peter rushed off. They wanted to catch the thieves. James was afraid to stay behind alone, so he was forced to follow them.

John had recognized the men. Three of them had come to California together with him, so he wouldn't let them get away with stealing from him.

It was late in the afternoon when they caught up with them. They were camping for the night. At first they were happy to see John Bidwell, but they became embarrassed when they learned about the reason for the visit.

Peter and James had been standing behind John with their rifles ready. Nothing seemed to be happening, though, so they put the rifles down and shared in the evening meal with the horse thieves.

"We needed a horse and a mule. We didn't know who owned them. We didn't think it mattered so much because there were so many of them," they apologized.

Peter could feel that they had great respect for John.

Later John Bidwell wrote about the journey and about Peter Lassen in his book *Journey in California*:

> He was a very lonesome man, also an ambitious man, a bit of a genius and very interested in the pioneer life—almost too much so! He trusted himself implicitly when the problem was finding a way through the wilderness, but on the way home he did make one mistake. When we passed Mount Butte Lassen claimed that we had to turn south, while I maintained that we had to go east. The end of our discussion was that we went in

different directions, and I reached home one day ahead of Lassen, who got lost in a swamp full of mosquitoes, where he was forced to spend the night.
I don't believe he ever forgave us.
But he was a man with many good sides. He was an excellent cook when you were camping, and he spared no efforts when he felt that others were willing to help him also. But if he discovered that someone cheated, he became angry and as grumpy as only a Dane can be. But this usually meant that everybody was ready to take their turn, and more was not necessary. Then Lassen would chase us all away and do the whole job himself. He even put up the tents for all of us.

When Peter came back to Sutter's Fort he immediately applied for a grant, a state grant, on the land by Deer Creek through General Manuel Micheltorena, the Mexican governor of California.
He applied for as much land as he could get. When he finally received his state grant, it had become five square-leagues, twenty-two acres.
Peter wasn't very patient. To pass the time before everything was settled, he moved his cattle to Cosumnes River. Here he built a house.
Sutter was not happy with the fact that Peter had moved away from the fort. But Peter wouldn't give in. He needed to get away from all the people in the fort. He wanted to go into solitude—out there in the untouched nature.

Ten

"California is a true paradise. I am not going back. I will never go east again. Here will be many towns. I can found one town after the other if I want to. Everything is here. California is a lovely country." Peter had gotten a spark in his eyes and he looked challengingly at the young Dutchman who had traveled with him from Sutter's Fort. "You, Sargent, come with me! I have found a good spot where we can build a house for the time being. There is sufficient pasture for the cattle. There is lots of wildlife."

The freckled Dutchman smiled. "I think you find good spots all the time wherever you want to found your towns. You speak about towns all the time. But okay, I'll come with you. It is getting monotonous here by Sutter. I believe that man is crazy anyway. There is something tiring about him. He is always bragging. You have done your part to make his fort bloom. You have forged and done repair work. You have made chairs and tables for everybody, and you have been hunting with the Indians to gain their trust and make them peaceful."

Peter shrugged. "I like to hunt with the Indians. They know what they are doing. They are clever hunters and they don't talk much. Furthermore, Sutter has Indians living at the fort. They obey him well enough."

The red-haired Dutchman got up and shook his long freckled body into place. He said, "Yes, but it is you they adore. Where was it you said this fine place is where we are going to settle down?"

Peter jumped up. "Look, it is by an eastbound subsidiary

stream to San Joaquin River. The river is called Cosumnes River."

Then Peter left with all his cattle and, together with Sargent, he went to Consumnes River.

It was summer, and California was young and fertile and full of promises.

During the fall the house was finished.

The summer had been good. The cattle were breeding well, and Sargent made butter and cheese from the milk.

It was obvious that Sargent was missing something. He was used to drinking a lot, and he loved women.

Peter sometimes asked himself how long Sargent could cope with him. They got on well together. But maybe Sargent thought that he was a little boring; he sometimes disappeared for several days to go hunting. It also happened, sometimes, that Peter became preoccupied with a certain matter, and at those times he completely forgot Sargent's presence.

Peter was hunting together with some Indians, who had a camp close by. He had also begun trading with them. The Dutchman was afraid of the Indians. Therefore Peter was surprised when he learned that Sargent had been visiting with them. He went there all the time.

Then one day, there he was with two young Indian girls.

"Look here what I have—two squaws for us."

Peter looked both confused and angry, when Sargent said, "They are going to keep house for us—one for each of us. That's good, isn't it?"

Peter mumbled something. His companion had a unique, irresistible charm. He was in his late twenties and his skin was tanned, but his teeth were unusually big and white. There was something fresh and convincing about his whole attitude. He slapped the nearest girl on the back.

Peter shrugged and said indifferently, "As you please."

Secretly he was wondering a little. The Indians had their

own rules for what women could do. Sargent must have used all his charm, or else he had given them some bullets to get permission to take away the two girls.

"They have to be back every evening. We can have them all day, but only to do work for us." Sargent was grinning. "We can do it in the daytime, too, can't we?" Happily he put his arm around one of the girls. Peter knew that the arrangement with the two girls meant that Sargent would last a while longer—maybe even all winter.

It wasn't that Peter feared the winter. He had experienced many winters, but the loneliness could sometimes make him wild and mad. He would manage by himself though.

With regard to the Indian girls, he wasn't morally condemnatory. Many settlers and gold miners took an Indian girl to live with them. There was a great need of women everywhere in California. Peter himself had never taken an Indian girl. He didn't feel it was dignified, and for that matter, members of her tribe could become difficult, especially if they believed they would soon be related.

He also felt a little sorry for the quiet dark girls who served the boastful gold miners in every way. If the girls became pregnant, and that happened often, they usually strangled the babies right after birth. With a few of the tribes it was considered very bad to have half-breed children.

The Indian tribes up here were very interested in keeping their women home for their own.

"I can't figure out what their names are. This one, and she is mine, is called something like Little Sun. So I call her Sun. The other one is called something with a bird. Call her Dove. You are better at the Indian language than I am. Or ask her yourself, or call her whatever you want."

Peter was a little annoyed with Sargent's tone of voice. It was obvious that Sargent didn't regard them very highly. Peter left the girl standing there and went over to the fireplace. He had been brought out of his circles. Did he respect them himself?

Since the battles in Keytesville, he had had some guilt feelings towards them. They were dangerous and savage in those days in Keytesville. But the fights had been unequal. The whites had weapons, and there were enough of them to take care of the Sioux Indians there. Ever since, wherever he would meet the natives Peter would try to talk to them. He had made great efforts to try and learn their language, and generally they respected him for it.

He took a poker fashioned by his own hand, and poked around in the burning coals. He felt nervous with the women around him here every day.

This thing with women was all in all something he couldn't really cope with, something that couldn't fall into place in his mind. Regitze was fighting within him as a fist against a darkened window. Regitze, whom he never understood. Regitze, who had been distant and near to him at the same time. Regitze, with whom he had been close for just a second. He was a hopeless romantic and couldn't do anything about it. It had only been natural that he in his loneliness, without relatives in Copenhagen, had fallen in love with her. He had had a great need to fall in love during those sad days. Anyone would have fallen in love with Regitze. Anyone young would have felt something for her anyway. He did not need to feel rejected when she married someone else, but he did anyway.

His experiences with women were not great. In Boston he had bought a woman just to try sex.

In Keytesville he had had a married woman. She slept with him to get a little relief from her much older and boring husband. She didn't really care about her little lover. Peter knew this all too well and felt badly about it. No, love was not for him. He was too small. He was nice-looking enough, but he was lacking something anyway. He was full of desires. He was burning for love and eroticism. When he suffered, he would rush out into the desert to hunt. He got up before everybody else and started to work. He was nice and helpful toward everybody. He wanted everybody to like him. Everybody would say that he was clever with his hands. But he felt cheated. Once he had made love with his soul and twice with his body. To combine soul and body was not possible for him. He didn't want to buy girls anymore. He didn't care for rented love. Some men got it for free. The married ones had it every day and every night. When they felt like it, they could just reach out their arm and they had their woman. For some it was easy, but not for him. His self-confidence disappeared when it came to women.

Sometimes he wished that it was possible to just once combine body and soul, to just once try the right and the incredible. His only comfort was that there were others in his situation. Monks, sailors, and Catholic priests had no women either; you could live without them and make good in so many other ways.

When he was riding in the mountains in the uncompromising sunbeams or sitting by the fireplace at night listening to his own breathing, he used to think that it had to be a man's right to have love, to be loved, to have sex. It had to be the right of every human being to give life to one single child in the world—a child he could bring up, one who looked like him and had his name. The pain in the palms of his hands came back, this pain in the hands that he couldn't explain. Even though he wasn't religious anymore, he often thought about when Jesus was spiked to a cross through the palms of his hands. Palms are so vulnerable.

Then came Sargent with these women. Even though they were only Indian women, they were created just like all other women, and that worried him. He was poking impetuously in the fireplace. The fire started burning again for a short while, and then it died out completely.

   Slowly he turned around and looked at Dove. She was just a child, he thought, astonished. So little and so dark and so firm. She had the characteristic broad, closed Mongolian face, cut off from the rest of the world, closed in within herself. She didn't give anything away. Her eyes were very narrow. She had an obvious Mongolian fold by the eyes, and the nose was completely flat, but her small mouth was beautiful and firmly closed. She wore a fur poncho and long boots. Her hair was long and braided, as the girls usually wore their hair around here, and she wore a beautiful pearl ribbon around her forehead.

   A little sister, he thought, quite relieved.

Eleven

The girls came every day and tidied the house for them. They washed clothes and cooked. As soon as Peter was out in the open, Sargent was busy making up to Suṅ. Peter had the feeling that Sargent need not strain himself very much, for the girl was apparently very interested in him. Very soon, a certain congenial intimacy arose between them, the kind of contact existing between people having an amorous relationship, an invisible string.

Peter told himself that this was indeed not his problem. Yet he was uneasy about it; and he took up a more and more unsympathetic attitude to the other girl, whom Sargent had so generously provided for him.

Sargent blamed him for his sourness toward her. "It's really a damned shame that you ignore her like this."

"She is a mere child, and I don't court Indian girls," Peter snapped, "but obviously there are others doing that."

Sargent did not reply but whistled complacently.

The atmosphere in the cabin began to get bad. The mild Californian winter rolled on with rain and snow-broth in the mountains. Dove came and went. She walked around softly on silent moccasins and did her job. Peter watched her furtively. He knew a bit of her language, and now and then he tried to explain to her something about her work or about what he was doing himself. She was apparently very interested in everything that he was doing and in his implements.

Her face was always totally closed when he spoke with her, but he knew that she was listening.

The Indians in these parts were very formal in their association with strangers. They were never spontaneous and never forgot their dignity. The only thing that could make them depart from this aloof reservedness was war. In war, one must expect anything. Their wildness could be violent and brutal.

The Indians were at their worst when they were in combat with the whites. Peter had made the observation that in their mutual wars they complied with an unwritten law preventing them from killing too many of the enemy warriors. The tribes could not bear to lose too many adult males. Most of their reciprocal warfare consisted of rapid attacks with yelling and hullabaloo. A large part of the battle involved the many preparations and the deliberation on strategy.

Peter greatly respected their consideration for the number of grown-up men and for the number of warriors in the tribe that could be dispensed with. Peter was full of wonder. This kind of consideration was not known by the whites.

Gradually Peter grew accustomed to Dove, and he looked at her wistfully in the evening when she tiptoed off in the dark on noiseless moccasins, to find her tribal kinsfolk behind the pine trees. Already in the afternoon he began to dread the moment when she produced her long shawl, the sign that she was about to leave. It hurt him when he stood by the fence and saw her disappear among the trees. She walked so neatly on her short legs, and she always held her shawl together with her right hand.

Then the rains finished, and the hot Californian summer came along. Sargent was away for long periods. Peter was bored. Sargent's girl was with child and she did not come every day.

Peter asked her in her own language what her kinsfolk thought of her being pregnant. She shrugged her shoulders. "There are other half-breed children in the tribe." She added that she wanted to get married. "But Sargent will not," she said quietly. "Yet he has promised me that I shall always be his Sun."

Peter wondered about these trappers who could travel here and there, begetting children with the Indian girls and remaining indifferent. After all, they were their children—their offspring. Sargent did not care now. It was a good thing, though, that apparently the tribe did not take the business with the child too hard.

On a hot summer day, Peter walked down to the river to cool off. It was too hot to work or to do anything at all, for that matter. But something else drove him as well. For he was sure that Dove had also gone to the river.

He walked along the bank. From his house he was able to watch the river, but the ford was situated behind a small group of pines. Sure enough—there she stood out in the stream, washing his clothes. She was naked. He sat down heavily on a rock by the riverside. The pine wood and the mountains lay behind him. Everything creaked remotely in the dry midday sun. A stone rolled down a hillside, and the sound was so strangely arousing in the arid stillness.

The California condor circled over the mountain behind the pine wood. A faint column of smoke reminded him of the presence of the Indians.

She was one with the landscape. She was a piece of young and sound America—California!

He could not help looking at her, the little tanned and sturdy figure out there in the cool water. She was short-legged and broad-hipped, but her tummy was flat and firm, and her small breasts were pointed and very provocative. They quivered slightly at her movements. Her long black hair flowed down her back. He noticed that she had no pubic hair. Most Indian women have few hairs on their body; they have neither pubic hair nor hair in the armpits.

How lovely and alluring she was. He could not tear himself away. His head felt giddy. Imagine, to experience it properly, to just once have the true experience—not paid love, not a stolen hour with someone else's wife. No, only once to possess a woman who was really his. At the same moment he thought, *She is only an Indian, isn't she?* But she was no longer just any Indian. She was Dove! Maybe he had fallen in love with her the first time he saw her, small and unapproachable, in the cabin.

She saw him, but did nothing to hide. On the contrary, she straightened herself as if in a state of well-being and walked with the washing basket on her hip closer to the place where he was sitting. When she was just opposite, she turned her back on him and stooped to rinse the laundry one further time. She stood with her legs apart, and he could see her behind and her genitals—they were immediately opposite him. He could not go on! The girl in the stream. The sun reflected in the water. Everything was shimmering before his eyes. He was sick with longing and lust. All the lonely nights, all the hammer strokes, all the implements he made, and all the knives he whetted; he toiled and moiled in order to forget his tormenting desire. For years he had been carried to and fro by the merciless craving and yearning.

He was breathing heavily. He was being carried away by his lust. He yearned ardently for the young firm body out there in the sun shimmer that flowed about her like streams of gold and boundlessness.

He plunged into the water. He did not give heed to his clothes getting wet. He would give everything away for a single joyous instant. He clutched her small bronze body, lifted her up, and carried her on to the river bank. He laid down heavily on top of her and realized that his wet clothes were in the way. With trembling hands he tore them off, so that his shirt buttons flew right and left. Again he threw himself upon her and thrust his member into her without having caressed her body. A twinge of pain was apparent in Dove's face, and he felt a gleam of guilt before he came—inside her.

She was silent during the whole act and did not reflect pleasure or lust, nor did she show any dislike.

For a while he lay on her, amazed at himself. He raised his head and looked down into her face. Her narrow eyes were firmly shut. "Sorry," he mumbled, feeling infinitely crude. He got up and offered her both his hands, in order that she might also get up.

There was a slight twitch around her eyes before she opened them. Reluctantly she took his hands, and he pulled her up. He led her to the river, where he plunged into the cool water. She walked with him diffidently into the shallow water. Here she squatted and washed her crotch. He noticed a very fine red flow running down her leg, mixing with the clear water. *She was a virgin,* he thought. *You were too hard and did not think of her at all.* She had marks from the stones on the river bank on her little round posterior. He walked up to her and helped her up. Then he stroked her hair. He was a short man and did not have to stoop very low to kiss her forehead. He turned her around and kissed the stone marks on her buttocks. Suddenly he felt better.

The girl turned and faced him, and a touch of a smile appeared on her face.

He suddenly laughed and said, "Dove, love!"

At a point farther down the river, a magnificent stag paced out to drink, and Peter was annoyed that he did not have his gun with him. California was a lovely country; the next time he would be more careful when he did it with her. At last, after so many years. Even though it was not perfect, it was a human being he held tight to himself, if only for a short while.

The California condor circled about the faint smoke column behind the pine wood.

Twelve

It had to come! One day the painful farewell had to come. He knew it all too well, that there always comes a farewell.

How many people have the possibility to follow each other through a long life? How many can in their old age pride themselves on having friends they have known all the way since childhood or youth? The harmonious married couple always says that they know each other completely. However, when the old couple are retired, only dusted towns and uncertain fantasies are left. The dream has become a heap of dead flowers that turn to dust when touched.

Peter was in doubt as to whether it was right to leave her behind, now that he was traveling to his ninety-eight square meters of land by Deer Creek. She was pregnant and the journey was long. He felt that it would be better to fetch her later. Things had to be put into a system first, and he also needed time to build a house. On the other hand, she was used to sleeping on the ground. She was strong and made no demands.

Changes! The inner and outer change—nobody could run away from himself, and nobody could stay within himself either. Everything was change. Even he himself was subject to change.

One morning he was standing there with all his cattle—his wealth—ready to go far away from Cosumnes River. He had gotten a grant, a state grant, on the land by Deer Creek. And she was standing there small and humble with big soft snowflakes in her black braids. She had gathered her shawl timidly around her narrow shoulders. She felt sad.

He looked at her and knew that she would be faithful to him. Dove wouldn't run away with just any goldminer passing by. Peter had started visiting her in her camp, and they seemed to accept him. None of her tribesmen had mentioned the baby she was expecting.

Peter liked children, including the Indian children he used to meet everywhere in the camp. He often took time to speak with them and teach them a little about tools and about how to treat them. There was, however, something inside him which rejected the child she was going to have. This child would never really be his. Even if he fetched her and raised the child among whites, it would always be a half-breed. This child would never be recognized among the whites. He knew their contempt. But could he accept the child himself?

In a way he was looking forward to this child, and in a way it was an embarrassment for him. The settlers would shrug at him if he seriously took care of this half-breed. He was bewildered. Of course he would fetch her. He had made her a promise. He saw doubt in her eyes. Didn't she believe him?

She was, however, the only one he had ever held close in the right way, the only human being who had ever given him warmth. A child could give him warmth, too.

This farewell was heartbreaking. Here she was in the soft snow freezing in her leather poncho. Her small hands holding the shawl together over her breast were trembling from the cold and sadness. Like him, she was small. That much they had in common.

He reached out for her, but she pulled back and examined him with her narrow eyes. It dawned on him that she was wise. He had never thought about that before. She *was* wise.

He took one step forward and put his arms around her

for a short moment, and then it was all over.

Sargent had trouble keeping the cattle steady.

"Farewell," he said and walked towards his saddled horse.

She tiptoed away without a sound on her soft leather soles.

He was busy taking care of the cattle, and when he took the time to look after her, she was already far away, on her way back to her tribe in the mountains. She was walking out of his life. She was looking down at the ground while she was walking, and suddenly with her hunched shoulders she looked even smaller.

The loose snow was lying soft over the rocks and the coniferous trees. For a short while the world was white and quiet. The howling and the stamping of the cattle came from far away—from a completely different time.

Without a sound she disappeared timidly up the stony road, away, far away, to a world he had never shared—her world.

Thirteen

Peter was on his way to Deer Creek, where the new dream land should be. This town, which so many settlers in California had needed, was going to be right here. Everything was to be put together here in Peter's hands.

Never stay too long; always go on, away from the present. His life was a hunt for the dream. He only dabbled in reality for the purpose of planning.

Peter was a little undecided about what he should call his new property. However, he decided quickly enough that it would probably be easier to found a town if he named it something Mexican. By the way, he was a Mexican citizen now. He would call the place Bosquejo Rancho, the wooded estate. The place had everything that any settler could dream of: lots of wildlife, salmon in the river, plenty of pasture for the cattle, and there was the forest, where one could collect timber for the building of houses.

Sargent didn't make it to Bosquejo Rancho. The small fanatic Dane got on his nerves. There were too many cattle to take care of, too many flooded rivers along the way. They had to wait weeks to get across. *Lassen has too many plans*, Sargent thought. *He is incredibly helpful, irritating in his persistence, and at times impossible to talk with.*

Sargent promised Peter to come to Bosquejo Rancho when Peter had founded his town, because Sargent wanted to be one of the first to move into the luxury hotel of the town. Of course it had to be equipped with lots of girls. Sargent talked himself nicely out of the partnership with Peter. Seemingly, Peter didn't care. He could make it on his own. It sounded like he meant it. Sargent was wondering. That man had never needed anybody, not even the little Indian girl. He hadn't been really kind to her. Why in the world didn't he bring the girl along? She was tough and very helpful, and she was expecting his child.

Sargent tried to forget about his own girl. He explained to himself and Peter that she was sloppy and hard to get along with. No, Sargent would turn back to Sutter's Fort, and later on it might prove lucrative to look for gold further north.

And then Sargent disappeared with a clean conscience.

Peter built on his "wooded estate," and the Indians helped him. He was the only white man for miles around. He learned their language and helped them with practical things. He taught them how to use tools.

In the beginning, the Indians looked after the cattle. Peter soon found out, though, that it was better to make fences; later he made use of the cattles excrement for fertilizing the fields. This was something new and aroused curiosity; the results were splendid. Peter grew both cotton and grapes for wine.

His hospitality was well known. For those who had made the long journey across the prairie, Bosquejo Rancho was a good place to gather strength before continuing on.

Two settlers, Ezekiel Merett and Charles Moon, visited him, and Peter made them aware of some rocks he had found by a small creek. These rocks would make very good grindstones. He named the place Stone Creek.

The two men were very excited and transported the stones on their mules to a punt down by the main river. Everything paid off well, and Peter bought cattle.

People began building houses on his land, and he sold land to those who wanted to build. He applied for more land from the Mexican government, but his application was denied.

Peter was happy in his new surroundings. Everything was shaping up. Time passed. Someplace Dove had hidden. He rejected her. Well, some time he could pick her and the baby up. He assumed her own took good care of them. Maybe she was still waiting for him? He rejected the thought. From time to time, he visualized her small curved back as she quietly walked up the mountain road with the shawl around her shoulders. What if she didn't wait, but married one of her own? And then what about the little half-breed?

"But I do care for you, Dove," he said to himself when he was working in the field.

All the time new Indians were coming to the area around Deer Creek. They lived on Peter Lassen's land, and they were not particularly grateful for that privilege.

The Indians living around him, he knew very well. He spoke their language, and daily they would come to him with their tools, or they would come to talk about something that was on their minds at the time.

But the new Indians, the Yanas, were not friendly. Several times they stole his cattle, and once they shot an arrow right past the head of one of the settlers on Peter's ranch.

However, the mountains remained in deep silence, and the sun had become a slice of warmth and confidence in the sky. In the afternoon it would cast its oblique and cool beams on the mountains and the treetops. Only a soft purl from the creek, looking for the river, could be heard. The birds would only caw reluctantly in the daytime, and they became completely quiet at sundown.

The trees around his large log cabin were swaying back and forth in secluded longing, and Peter Lassen's clock ticked away in the living room, telling that time passed and passed over the mountains in the noonday heat and in the cool nights.

When it rained in the river, the pine trees would drip on the many deer, who like mirages moved through the forest on their way to find water to drink. Sometimes the silence would be broken by cattle who would low and tremble uneasily inside their fencing.

When the travelers came with their wagons and their exhausted animals, Peter would get busy. When they left again, he would suck in the silence and go up in the mountains to hunt.

More and more people came to Lassen's ranch, and one day no less than fifty soldiers with horses and mules came. They were under the command of Colonel John Charles Frémont and Kit Carson. Peter was glad and worried at the same time at getting so many guests all at once. Now he had to get all the settlers working, because so many different things were needed to serve so many.

There were also others, however, who became worried by the sight of so many—the Yana Indians! They tiptoed along the river and looked at the strangers with crooked unfriendly eyes.

One day some of Frémont's horses disappeared, and a couple of days later a settler was lying dead on the road leading up to Peter's house. The settler had a big wound in his chest; the arrow had been torn out and removed, but there was no doubt among the settlers as to who was behind the killing—the Yanas!

Peter called in his Indian helpers and asked them to spy on the Yanas to find out what they were up to.

"My people are in danger here. We also risk losing more of our riding horses. Peter Lassen, this is your land, and you are responsible for our security," Frémont said accusingly.

He and Kit Carson sat at the wooden table together with Peter in the living room of the wooded estate. Peter looked admiringly at the elegant man opposite the table. Frémont's brown hair was neatly curled at his ears, his beard was trimmed and very well groomed, and he was very tall.

Frémont appreciated Peter very much. They had met earlier at Sutter's Fort. There Peter had met his wife, too. She looked like Regitze.

Next to Frémont sat Kit Carson. He was more on the broad and common side. He had a sour expression around his mouth, and his grayish brown hair was shoulder-length. Peter enjoyed being with them. Frémont was busy measuring temperatures and drawing maps over the western areas. He was sent out by the US government to do this job.

"Isn't it possible to give these dogs a scare that will keep them quiet for a little while?" Kit Carson asked, as he emptied his beer mug.

"Do you want some more meat?" Peter asked.

"No thank you, Peter, you have taken good care of us. But what are we going to do about the Indians?" Frémont asked. "You know them best."

Peter was sitting peeling meat off a bone without really thinking about what he was doing. He wished they would leave the Indians alone. On the other hand, the savages had never before killed settlers around here. It was those damned Yanas, why couldn't they have walked around his estate, and why did they come now, when he had such fancy visitors?

A mild wind blew in through the open door. "How about closing the door?" Frémont said. "One never knows what they might think of. You never hear them until it is too late."

Peter sighed, turned the lamp up a little and looked towards the open door which was placed in the wall like a piece of cut-out night. All of a sudden a stone came rolling down the hill in front of the house.

Kit Carson jumped up from the wooden bench and ran toward the wall for his rifle. Peter had never feared open doors or the lonesome nights at campfires. There was somebody outside. He could hear the footsteps. Peter knew that his hearing was better than most people's, and he knew that there was only one person outside the house and that person was wearing moccasins. It was no doubt one of his own Indians. He turned around and looked at the door. "Don't shoot," he said in a tone of authority to Kit.

From the square night-hole in the wall an Indian shadow came sliding in. Peter recognized it. It was one of his cattle watchmen.

"What's new?" he asked.

The Indian answered quietly, "The Yanas are busy. They are preparing for a great battle. They are dancing war dance at nighttime."

"Oh," Peter said, and he stared intensely at the Indian. "Do they have their women and children with them in the camp?"

"No, only warriors. Their camp is further up the river on the opposite side. I can show the way. You can hear them far away."

Peter dismissed the Indian, and he disappeared through the night-square.

Kit Carson turned back to the table, and for security reasons he brought his rifle with him. "I'll be damned if I will let my people be massacred by that riffraff."

Frémont added, "There is no doubt, that we have to attack fast. You know the area, so you must help us, Peter."

Peter respected Frémont and admired his elegant and fine manners, but most of all he respected the systematic way he worked, measured, make maps, took temperatures— everything was done with the utmost accuracy. Frémont was a learned man, a man who was never in doubt as to what he wanted when he went someplace. Sometimes Peter felt sad that he wasn't very educated. Furthermore, Frémont had a lovely wife who looked like Regitze.

Peter had become very generous toward the Indians. He didn't like to kill them anymore. They were as good settlers as the white people. They were just brought up to do things differently. They had different beliefs than the white people. After his acquaintance with Dove, he couldn't really fight them anymore. Of course he realized that the situation was a little dangerous now. If they were really going to do the war dance, well, then they did have something in mind.

Frémont demanded that he do something.

"Okay then, let us take them by surprise and give them a little scare. We should be able to handle that. We need not actually cut them down," Peter said.

Kit Carson got an unpleasant look in his eyes that disturbed Peter, and he felt troubled about the whole thing.

"What is your plan?" Frémont asked.

Peter looked speculatively into the lamp on the table. "I have some large rafts and some small boats. We can sail the men across the river and then surprise them, shoot a little, and chase them away."

"Good, Peter, you show the way, because you know the river and how far we are going. It is very important that we be put ashore some distance from the camp. They mustn't be able to hear us."

Kit was already on his way out into the night. He shouted outside the house, "I'm gathering people now. And you, Peter, you have some good Indians we can use!"

Peter left the security of his warm house with the wooden table and led them up the river on the rafts. They sailed back and forth many times to get everybody across to the opposite bank. During the night the clouds spread and the full moon came out. It cast its white and stagnant light over the river and over the men, who were working in the shelter of the night.

The Indians were dancing a war dance! If they hadn't been dancing, they would have noticed the vibrations from the many feet moving on the ground. But they didn't suspect anything.

Peter, Frémont and Kit Carson divided the people in

such a way that the camp would be surrounded.

Kit Carson gave a sign when everybody was in place. The Yanas were taken completely by surprise. The white soldiers came from all directions, and they shot at every Indian who stepped out into the moonlight. The sky became more and more cloudless, and Peter could see that his Indian scout had lied to him. There were women and children in the camp.

The children crawled into the tents. A minute later some burning torches were thrown after them, and the tents were on fire. Something twisted, hurt someplace in Peter's stomach, or was it in his joints? They were burning the children! And he had led the soldiers here. Why couldn't anybody be trusted?

A young woman ran across the square with her small child in her arms. A soldier fired a shot at the child, and she ran screaming into a burning tent. One minute later she came out like a burning torch. Holding the child, she disappeared into some bushes on the opposite side of the camp.

Peter wanted to follow her but his legs wouldn't obey him. The square was full of screaming Indians. They were running around like living torches. The tents were burning, and he could hear the children screaming inside of them. The shots echoed in the mountains, while the pine forest stood silent and dark around the camp.

He walked toward the river. Everything had slipped away from him. He sat down on a rock and looked at the moonlit water. All this suffering—it was hard to endure. He hoped it would soon be over. A torch ran past him and jumped in the cool river. A little later a burnt and hateful Indian came out of the water. He stood there for a little while swaying in the moonlight, his torso was black and bleeding, his dark and evil look burnt into Peter's mind. He shouted in Indian language which Peter understood, "I remember you! You will bleed for this night."

He jumped back into the river, and a little later he was just a dark shadow on the opposite bank.

When the morning came, the Indian camp was just a smoking heap of ashes.

The white people sailed back on their rafts to Bosquejo Rancho.

They were tired but pleased that they had "given them a scare." Now there would be peace for some time, they thought.

Peter remained. Yes, peace was secured on his ranch, and Kit Carson and Frémont agreed that they had done Peter a favor by establishing peace in this place.

In the early morning light he went up into the dark pine forest, lay down on his back between the tall trees and mumbled, "Dove, I must see you again. I must fetch you. I cannot be sure that you are alright in the camp."

He visualized the young woman from last night—a frail torch disappearing into the bushes—and the child who, scared to death, pressed his head against her. He should never have left Dove. He could see her, the small timid creature walking slowly, and with her back curved, up the mountain path without looking back.

He would go to Consumnes River to fetch her.

Only one survived the killings in the Indian camp. That was the torch who jumped into the river and swore revenge.

Fourteen

Peter went back to the Consumnes River. The peace of the afternoon hung light and hostile between the mountains. The pine trees were silent but the river purled softly, and every time the horse's hooves hit a stone or made the gravel move, it sounded unpleasant and harsh in the silence.

He passed his empty house and continued up the mountain road toward the Indian camp.

He was hoping for a good reception, even though he had only been in the camp a few times. Would they accept him? Suddenly he could not wait any longer. He was longing to see Dove. He could not wait to see his own child. The child would be around one and a half years old.

The horse was sweaty and tired because he had not rested at all that day. He wanted to see Dove.

He arrived! He dismounted and left the horse walking around. He looked and looked but saw nothing—the camp was gone!

First he saw the tall grass. It was very sparse up here in the mountains. The grass was moving back and forth in the light wind. They apparently moved on. He could not understand it. For years they had their camp here. They once told him that they were afraid to get too close to the whites. They were happy with the area by Consumnes River because it was very seldom that any strangers came, at the most a few fur-hunters. The camp was also well protected by the mountains and the pine forest.

The fingers of the sun became long and narrow, and the

shadows from the mountains slid like mud down the hills.

His sweaty horse walked peacefully around, eating the long, thin grass. He began to have a closer look between the grass stalks, and his midriff became tired and heavy. Between the straws he saw black ashes. He saw faintly the contour of a tepee. He walked further and saw the next black contour of a tepee in the grass. He continued on and discovered burnt black wooden pieces. He knew what had happened. The tents had been burnt down. He walked around and found pieces of earthen cookware, burnt tools, and leather pieces.

How long ago did this happen?

For a long time he just stood there looking. Exactly the same thing happened here as at his own ranch—the total destruction!

Who did this?

He was being pulled toward the end of the camp. In between the long thin straws, a heap of granite boulders lay together like some kind of cairn. A small humble wooden cross was planted in it.

He was mourning—some Godfearing person put a wooden cross in the cairn.

He stood there for a little while in front of the silent monument. With hesitating blacksmith hands he removed some of the outer stones. A long cold sunfinger found its way into the hole and he discovered one charred cranium after another. The empty eyeholes looked past him out into the freedom, and the smoked teeth were smiling without presence.

He sat at the cairn until night fell and the moon cast its white light over the granite boulders.

He wanted to shout out her name, but no one knew better than he that the sorrow of the human being is nothing to nature. He knew that the murders at Bosquejo Rancho were avenged here at Consumnes River. And he also knew that no one would ever be able to tell him if he had a daughter

73

or a son in this camp. A cold cairn full of dead black shadows was the only witness he had.

In the morning he found his horse and went back to Bosquejo Rancho.

Fifteen

People and states often sacrifice themselves to ruin or destruction by their inability to agree.

The governor of California, Pio Pico, did not agree with General José Castro. The general gathered the Mexican troops to go against the many American immigrants in the northern part of California.

And Peter Lassen and Frémont worked frantically to gather troops, horses, and supplies.

On the surface, however, it was William B. Ide, Henry L. Ford, and Ezekiel Merrit who were the active ones.

Although Peter was in the woods, he was everywhere organizing. And one day California became part of the USA. Over Sonoma Garrison the bear flag was swaying. One morning, the 14th of June 1846, a flag was hoisted over the garrison's square tower, a piece of white cotton material upon which a bear was placed, cut out of a red flannel shirt, the thirty-first star in the Stars and Stripes. The flag was up for about a month, and then it was replaced by the Stars and Stripes.

T. Vogel-Jørgensen writes in his book *Peter Lassen of California*:

> The chief of the American navy, Commander—later Admiral—John Drake Sloat, went ashore in Monterey on the second of July and conferred here with counsel Larkin, who showed Sloat his instructions from President Polk and tried to convince the navy chief that what was

happening in California was a step on the way toward the separation of the country from Mexico and the incorporation into the USA. After five days he succeeded in convincing Sloat: The seventh of July he went ashore with a small army and hoisted the American flag over Monterey and declared the capital and the country as a US territory—before the single states of the USA were recognized and incorporated as states, they were as a rule for a period of time, territories—which determines a preparation phase.

The war, which was now a reality, developed in different ways, and the war was rather bloodless in California. The Americans moved into one city after the other—General Kearney on the tenth of January 1847 in Los Angeles, which Lieutenant Gillespie had seized for some time . . . Then the Mexicans gave up. On the fourteenth of January, Frémont arrived—he was active all over as soon as the war was official—in Los Angeles with a happy announcement. The day before, a cease-fire had been made between Frémont, who had four hundred men behind him, and General Andrés Pico, the chief of the Mexican National Army in California. In this treaty Mexico recognized the loss of California.

Commander Stockton came shortly after, on board the cruiser *Congress*, to Monterey directly from the USA with fresh action orders. He was to take command, which Sloat reluctantly gave him in Monterey. In reality it was intended that Stockton should come and conquer California—but this had already been taken care of!

All in all the war lasted one year.

California had become American, and now was the time for Peter to found a real town on his land. He would name it Benton City, named after Frémont's wife, because she looked like Regitze.

Sixteen

Peter was hunting in the mountains. However, he had not caught anything for several days.

The snow fell heavily; soon it would be nighttime. He'd better find his way back to the small cottage he was living in when he hunted around here.

Suddenly Benton City had become unbearable. Sometimes he felt strangely empty and tired inside. Then he couldn't speak with anyone, not even listen. When he felt like this, he could not do any practical work.

Peter felt best when he had big plans. He would become tired and heavy and full of disinclination every time the adventure was over. Deep down inside he always felt a little sad. The settlers liked the things he was making with his hands. They were impressed with all the things he could do, but the man himself, the small broad man and all his strength, they found very uninteresting. The people he felt close to sooner or later disappeared out of his life. Here in the wintertime, when the others were happy inside their houses, he felt a strange transfiguration about life.

He walked firmly in his snowshoes along the mountain road. The snow was lying thick all over, even on the needles of the pine trees. They were heavily burdened by the snow.

The moist peace did him good. The snow was so high that he did not have to be afraid of bumping into rocks and rough spots on the surface with his snowshoes.

While he walked with his rifle over his one shoulder and the hunting bag over the other, he thought about how he could get hold of more people for his town. This thought had long been circling around in his head, but now he knew what he wanted. He would travel far east and find immigrants whom he could then bring back over the prairie and make sure that they settled in his town. He was figuring on going all the way to Missouri. Here he could also ask permission to found a Masonic lodge in Benton City. That would give the town respectability.

It started to get dark then, but Peter was never afraid to walk alone in the mountains. He mapped them and gave names to lots of the roads and localities. He put up road signs and markers everywhere, to help the travelers find their way.

It was completely dark when he reached his hunting cottage. Already in the distance he could see that somebody was there. There was smoke coming from the chimney, and a dim light could be seen in the small window. It had been several days since Peter saw a human being. Could it be an Indian? They usually didn't go into the houses. But if they did go in, it was most likely to find food or tools.

Peter stepped out of his snowshoes and put them carefully up against the wall of the cabin, then he took the gun down from his shoulder and kept it ready for safety. Then he kicked open the door and looked around the room.

By the small wooden table, a man was sitting and eating. It was nice and warm in the house, because a fire had been lit in the fireplace. Peter could smell that the man had fried some meat, but the meat on the table did not look very well fried.

The man was very thin and the meat in front of him was almost raw. *He must be very hungry*, Peter thought. "You have taken the meat that I had hanging outside the house," Peter said, carefully watching the man.

"Yes, I haven't had food for several days. I don't have any more bullets. It is difficult to get hold of game when one only has the possibility of catching it in traps and snares."

Peter took off his big fur coat. "Why are you running around here and starving, and where did you come from? You are not wearing enough clothes." Determined, Peter took away the meat from him and put it back on the frying skewer on the fireplace.

"You are going to be sick if you eat it raw," Peter said while rearranging the firewood.

The man was watching Peter with sunken hungry eyes. Then he said, "My name is James Reed. I'm on my way to get help. I was following a large caravan from the east. It hasn't arrived yet. I'm afraid that there has been an accident."

"Why are you not together with them?" Peter asked, looking questioningly at the man.

He moved over to a wooden block by the fire. He had obviously lost interest in the meat, and he reached his dirty and thin hands toward the heat. His shirt was torn, and there was a long tear in his leather trousers from the knee down.

"They branded me outlaw," he said quietly and looked at his frostbitten hands.

Peter was turning back to the present. The feeling of despair that had haunted him for several weeks was disappearing. He was back from the mountains and the sadness. The man in front of him had his full sympathy and interest.

"What a lot of nonsense. They can't do that," he said and waited anxiously for an explanation.

While the man was talking, Peter was looking after the frying skewer.

"You see, to start with there were twenty-nine of us coming from Springfield in Illinois. We wanted to go to California to find happiness." He breathed heavily. "And what have I found?" he mumbled.

"Go on," Peter said impatiently.

"I brought my wife and four kids along. The brothers

George and Jacob Donner were there too. We called the caravan "The Donner Party." More joined us all the time, and when we left Fort Bridger, we counted altogether eighty-seven. But right from the start there was trouble and disagreements because of a disgusting guy by the name of John Snyder. I couldn't stand him. He was bullying his wife and he beat up his children and his oxen. By the Great Salt Lake we had a dispute. There was a new road that could have taken us over the mountains and would have made the trip 480 kilometers shorter. Most of us preferred this road. But three of the men were stubborn, and they said that we should travel by the old caravan road. That one was safer, they said. The Donner brothers said no, and the three men traveled the old route alone.

"We were attacked by Indians, who stole most of the cattle. Before that some of the cattle had run away, because they were wild from thirst. When we finally reached Sierra Nevada, there was neither road nor path, and we couldn't figure out which direction to choose. We had several children with us in the caravan. Some of them were sick and tired, and our team of oxen had been greatly weakened.

"John Snyder became meaner and meaner during the trip. Nobody dared come near his wagon. His wife was scared and stayed inside the covered wagon whenever somebody came close.

"My four children did very well on the whole trip, and my wife was fantastic. She is such a wonderful human being. Every single night during the whole trip she said a prayer with the children. She helped the other women with their children, and if anybody got hurt, she was always ready to help.

"While we were fighting to find our way through the Sierra Nevada, John Snyder began to interfere in the way we drove our oxen. Up till now he had been whipping his own animals terribly. The poor oxen were moaning from pain, and the flies were sitting in the flesh wounds made by his whip in their backs. But now he started on the other people's animals. People were afraid of him, but nobody dared say anything. The big heavy wagons were hard to get over the rocks and up the mountains.

"Every time we thought we had found a good road, it ended up at a big rock or an impassable stretch of gravel and sand. One day John Snyder began whipping my oxen and I could hear how they were suffering. He seemed to think that they were going too slowly. I became so angry that I jumped down from my wagon, ran over to him, and told him to mind his own business. He was to stay away from my animals. My wife came down from the wagon too and stood by my side. And now—will you believe it—he lifted his big whip to hit her. I don't know if you have a woman, but if you do you would defend her against everyone. I wasn't thinking. I was so afraid that the whip would touch her.

"I pulled my knife and stabbed him. I didn't know where I stabbed him. I just wanted to stop his disgusting arm and the whip, which was red from the oxen's blood. I felt how the knife hit one of his ribs. It only lasted a short second, then it went deeper in and he fell.

"I just stood there; I couldn't make myself look to see what had happened. He was lying on a rock, and the blood was running down the stone. I was alarmed over what I had done, but I didn't care about him. He was a disgusting human being. The Lord does not want us to kill, but this man did not deserve to live. I hope God will forgive me for what I have done.

"The others from the caravan came over. He died in a couple of minutes. Afterwards there was a strange atmosphere. We made a stop. At first nobody knew what to do. But at last they buried John Snyder under a bunch of rocks and put a wooden cross there. One of the Donner brothers said a prayer. After that they had a trial. My defender helped me as much as he could, and everybody who had had trouble with John stood by my side. They agreed that the killing was understandable, but the trial determined that we people must not kill. It says so in the Ten Commandments. There were also some men who said that a murder is a murder, and therefore the one who kills should be executed.

"The Donner brothers settled the case, they branded me outlaw until the caravan reached California. If I could make it there on my own, well, then that was okay.

"Some of the men would have killed me if I didn't disappear right away. I wasn't allowed to take a weapon or a horse. After a while, they did let me take a horse, though. I disappeared in a hurry, and I barely had time to say goodbye to my wife and our children.

"And then something wonderful and strange happened. My little Virginia, twelve years old, came out to me in the middle of the night, along with my neighbor from Springfield, Milton Elliott, who was also with us in the caravan. My wife had talked Milton into taking Virgina with him, and they had found my trail.

"I received weapons and food from them. I held my little darling tight and promised her that we would soon meet again in California.

"Since then I have fought my way ahead. I came here, and I don't want to leave this area; I have a feeling that they are around here somewhere. If they have gotten through, that is. I do not believe that they—with their heavy wagons—could have made the trip faster than I have. I am afraid that something has happened to them. I was one of those who led the trip, along with the Donner brothers. I know they must have had a difficult time without me. I was better at finding our way from the map. Before we began this trip, I had gone through the route carefully in all its details.

"It is snowing now. The snow is too deep for those heavy wagons, and the oxen must be completely exhausted."

Peter looked thoughtfully at James Reed. He put the now completely well-done meat in front of him and said, "I know a good man. You can count on me. We will go to Benton City and fetch everything that we need for an emergency expedition." And not without pride he added, "That's my town."

But Reed was too occupied eating to hear the last sentence.

Seventeen

At Lake Tahoe there were a bunch of simple huts. They were covered by seven meters of snow. But there were people in the huts. In one of them was Mrs. Reed and two of her children. The twelve-year-old Virginia was alright, even though she was starving. The boy of five was also well, but the two little ones were tired and completely exhausted, and they were left in other huts not far away.

It was dark and cold in the huts. In Mrs. Reed's house a small fire was burning. The thick snow outside helped to retain the warmth from their bodies. There were also some bodies that were not radiating heat anymore. They were dead or dying.

All the oxen had been eaten, and soup had been made from their hides.

Mrs. Reed was thinking about the two little ones. She found it best to leave them, as everybody agreed that they could get help fast when Tahoe was reached. Yes, then it would be possible to find help and occupied places. She was aware that the cold could kill little hungry children. Therefore she regretted now that she didn't bring them along. She began to doubt that they had any chance.

Since her husband was forced to leave the caravan, everything went wrong. It was almost like the spirit disappeared with him. Until now she was the only one in the whole caravan who hadn't lost a child. But now her courage was finally disappearing. Here in the snow-covered huts, people were dying all around her. There were six to eight people in every hut, and she knew that at least five from their camp were dead.

She had no idea how the two little ones were doing, or anyone else for that matter. No one knew, either, whether the men and women who had taken off by themselves to get help had survived.

She was too tired and too hungry to cry. Their clothes were in a miserable state, and they were all very dirty and uncared for. Why did this have to happen with their caravan? Why couldn't their trip be a success? Others had traveled over the prairie and made it. Yes, in reality she could not imagine at all that the others before had as many accidents, Indian attacks, and deaths as their caravan. It was like John Snyder's evil spirit had ruined everything for them; yes, he had put a curse on the whole trip. Now she was faced with a new problem. In the neighboring hut they had begun to eat the dead bodies. They had no food and no chance to get out of the mountains in this snow. She could not get it through her head. How did this happen, that she, they, were sitting here in this situation? They had to either eat human meat or die from starvation. She felt that it was impossible, a sacrilege against God's creation. She simply could not do it. She looked at the children; they were so skinny and worn out. What if help came too late? She could keep the children alive with human flesh until help could come. The children had a long life ahead of them. Was it right to stop them from living? She thought on. *If we do not get saved anyway, then I will have this sin also to bring before God*. Because it was a sin to eat another human being. The children would be innocent in God's judgment; they were without guilt. She had to take the responsibility. She also knew that they would have to eat now, otherwise it would be too late. In a few days, the hunger would not be so hard anymore, they would become more and more tired and apathetic about everything, and then they would die. They had to eat while they still had the drive and the strength to fight for life. She thought on. *If we are rescued, can we then live with what we have done? Can we then live on with the unhappy knowledge about ourselves? Isn't death to be preferred to a life in guilt?* She folded her hands and prayed to God for mercy. She prayed for God to show her the right way.

She fell asleep and dreamt that she was walking up a mountain. There is a rumble in the distance like thunder. On top of the mountain there stood a shape in a golden cape. She could not see the face because a golden hut was pulled over the head of the shape. She was worried about the legs. They looked exactly like lizard legs, a little crooked and full of scales, and the feet looked like those of a lizard. The golden cape was beaming against a completely blue sky, and a light wind made the yellow limestones squeak. *"I AM,"* says the shape. *"I AM, no one must see my face. He who sees God's face shall die."*

"What am I to do?" she asked in despair. "I cannot eat another human being to live."

"Life is my gift to people. You have to be careful with life. Life is to be preferred to death. Everything in this world has two sides: light and shadow, night and day, life and death, love and hatred, good and evil. If we didn't know evil, how could we evaluate good? To know life, you must suffer. If you will not take your own life upon yourself, you have lost it. I once sent a man by the name of Jesus to you. They dragged a woman in front of him, a woman whom they condemned as a whore. Do you know what he said to her? 'I do not judge you, go away and sin no more from now on!' I do not condemn you either, go in peace."

She woke up and she felt quite at ease.

In the hut with her there were three older men and a young girl. They had lit a fire with a wooden coffin that one of them had brought inside. They were cooking meat.

She crawled over to them in the dim light. "Is that human

flesh that you are cooking?" she whispered.

They looked at her quietly and full of guilt. They had great respect for her.

She didn't want to see which one of the dead bodies they had cut the meat from. They had covered them up, even the one they had taken the meat from.

"Promise me you won't say anything to the children. Tell them that you found a dead rabbit outside the door." She gave them a pleading look. The dirty, hungry people looked over at the sleeping children. They nodded their heads.

On the way to Benton City, James Reed and Peter met some of the survivors from the Donner Party. They were able to explain where the huts with the others from the caravan were. James Reed was happy to learn that his wife and at least two of his children were alive. Peter was busy getting equipment and men for the rescue mission. Shortly after they found the snowed-in people.

Mrs. Reed and the two children were sent to Benton City and were quartered at Peter's house.

James Reed kept on searching for the two smallest children. He found them alive.

The Reed family was the only family in the caravan that made it to California all together.

James Reed and his family settled in San José, where they became very wealthy.

"The One who is called I AM has sent me to you" (Ex. 3:14).

Eighteen

"If you are from Honey Lake Valley, you can't get work—out there you get rich just by smoking your pipes while nature does the job. You learn not to work."

Peter had gone into the great Paiute chief Old Winnemucca's tent. He sought out Indians more and more, when he was out hunting or looking for new gold mines. As he grew older, he could see that the white man had made a mistake. Peter did not wish to judge. The white people did not really understand the Indians' way of thinking, therefore, they could never really reach them.

The other day, the following event was announced: "A goldminer noticed that an Indian he had met in the forest had an unusually good rifle. The goldminer tried to tempt the Indian to sell it for a big bag of gold. He succeeded only after many attempts, as Indians are not interested in gold.

"When the goldminer had gotten some distance away from the Indian with his new rifle, he shot him, and then he went back and took back his bag of gold."

Now Peter was sitting by the fire smoking a pipe. He said to Old Winnemucca, "I am founding a new town."

Old Winnemucca was not especially interested.

"Benton City never really amounted to anything. I have left my ranch in Indian Valley for good. I belong here in Honey Lake Valley. I will found a new town here. This time I will succeed. Maybe I will found a whole new state here in the valley. I have already found gold. Maybe not large quantities, but something. Why do I always miss the great luck?

There are not many goldminers here in the valley yet, but they will come. There is no doubt about it, and then there will be a need for a town where they can have all their needs taken care of."

Old Winnemucca puffed on his pipe and said, not without some hostility, "These prospectors have no brains. They take it all: the wild game, the earth, and the place for my people. I don't really understand what they are going to use the gold for. The whites here in California come from the other side of the world. They have bidden farewell to their tribes and hunting grounds to find small gold stones by the river. And if anyone takes these small stones, which we Indians don't think anything of, then they kill them to get back these worthless stones.

"Much has happened in my time. When I was a child we did not see any whites around these parts. You have also come from the other side of the world. What is your ancestors' country called?"

"Denmark—my town is named Farum," Peter replied. He had learned a little Paiute, and Winnemucca could speak a little English. They managed to communicate quite well together.

Peter said, "I have found a tree I want to die under, because I will not move anymore. I will die in Honey Lake Valley."

Winnemucca replied grandly, "You are talking about my ancestors' country. If you really want to, you are welcome to die on my parents' land."

"Strange thing about you Indians—you think you own everything. You always speak for each other, but never for yourselves."

To this Winnemucca said, "We cannot speak for ourselves because an Indian is never one, but a part of an ancestry and the land."

eastern boundary, from there east to the 117th western longitude, then north to the 42nd northern longitude (shall be the width) finally running towards the west to the 120th western longitude (northeast corner of California), thereafter south to the starting point.
The named territory shall be called Nataqua.
2. Any present male settler who is 21 years old shall have the right to claim an area of 640 acres.
3. Any person who claims an area has to put up an announcement about the size as accurately decribed as possible of the mentioned area, and also institute that the description is entered in the records.
4. All claimed areas have to be surveyed within ninety days from the day when the announcement is put up and notice given to the registrar, and the aforementioned survey, together with the entry in the records, has to be performed in the presence of the owner.
5. All possessions being claimed and surveyed this way have to be put into service by the owner or his substitute.
6. All land situated between Roop's house and the forest towards the west, and between the hills on the north side of Susan River and three hundred yards west of the Immigrant Road, Roop has to lay out for a town, and every settler has to be entitled to a building lot on this town area, provided that he effects a building being put up before the first of May A.D. 1857. All parts of the aforementioned town area which are not plut into service according to the stipulation in this paragraph have to belong to aforementioned Roop.

7. Any owner shall have the right to settle or to utilize either the town area or the possession, and the town area will then be regarded as an extension of his possession of 640 acres.
8. No person is allowed to lead streams from their original river beds when it can cause harm to any of the earlier owners of land.
9. All difficulties and all disputes have to be settled by arbitrators selected by the inhabitants of the valley, and decisions made by this arbitration will be final.
10. No person is allowed to sell, exchange, or, in any other way, hand out any kind of liquor to the Indians, and any person or persons who misuse, maltreat, rob, or steal from the Indians will be regarded as a lawbreaker, and at the request of any person who writes to the registrar that such an offense has taken place, the registrar shall without hesitation summon the citizens. They will make a court, and after having heard all circumstances they will determine and hand out such punishment as they find justified.
11. The registrar has to be chairman in any such court and has to keep a record of all negotiations in this court. In the absence of the registrar, a majority of the court will elect a chairman, and the majority will determine the procedure of the court.
12. A surveyor and a registrar will be elected to take care of their tasks until successors are elected and nominated.
13.–19. These deal with the building of new roads, which have to be thirty-three meters wide.
20. Isaac Roop is elected registrar and Peter Lassen is elected surveyor, and they shall both act in their respective offices from today.

21. We, the undersigned permanent residents of Honey Lake Valley, are obliged by honor one and all to faithfully comply with these laws and regulations and to hold on to them and defend them sacrosanctly.

Peter Lassen
president

Isaac Roop
secretary

Nineteen

The Atsugewi tribe would steal cattle from the whites in Honey Lake Valley, and the whites would attack in retaliation. Winnemucca's warriors, the Paiute tribe, helped the whites by fighting Atsugewi, because Paiute had never been able to get along with his archenemy, Atsugewi.

The white people quickly organized a corps to maintain control of the Indians in the area. Peter organized sixty men, consisting of ranch owners and their workers.

There was something about this war against Atsugewi that Peter didn't like. It had been much too hard. It was more than a simple disagreement. The Paiute Indians were becoming too savage. Their blood had been brought to a boil, but Winnemucca was seemingly uninterested in the dispute. He would sit in his tent, big and bare in his brown wrinkled skin, and think. "I feel that the final hour is close. I can sense that soon the soldiers will come and kill us. Something is on the way," he said thoughtfully to Peter, who had come to ask the old chief's advice.

"I have been appointed Indian agent," said Peter.

"What is that, if I may ask?" asked Winnemucca.

"The Indian agent is responsible for smoothing out the differences between the Indians and the whites. Furthermore, I am to help those Indians who have gotten into trouble."

"Old Peter Lassen, you are a good man who will only do what is good for us. I must tell you, though, that more blood will flow. While I was fighting Atsugewi, the Washoe tribe—whose war courage no one holds in especially high regard—attacked a ranch and stole some potatoes from its owner. I heard from one of my men that some whites are on their way. My warriors wish to help Washoe in this fight."

Peter looked scared at Winnemucca. "I thought that you and I agreed to help each other and never to steal from each other," he said, taking offense at this breach in faith.

"My warriors have their reasons to help Washoe," Winnemucca replied shortly.

"Washoe has naturally taken advantage of the fact that everybody is away from the town," Peter mumbled. "Where is this ranch situated?"

"Southeast of the town by the southwestern bank," Winnemucca replied as he put another log on the fire.

Peter left him in a hurry.

While Peter Lassen was in the Indian camp, Isaac Roop, M.C. Lake, and John Weikel had sent an urgent appeal for help to California's governor and asked him to send some soldiers.

When Peter heard this, he became angry, because he knew all too well what soldiers would mean to the Indians. Now was the time to act. The rumors said that Washoe also had set on the Maidutribe to participate in the fight against the whites. The Indians were apparently determined to wipe out all the whites in Honey Lake Valley. The reinforcement would mean killing and burnt-down tepees. Yes, he had seen it before. He had tried hard to look past the place in his mind called Dove. He knew that life could not be relived, that time goes, and that it goes faster and faster the older he got. No, he could not really cope anymore. He just knew that California was the land he chose, and the land that became his destiny. Denmark with the many light beech trees and the light nights was not the place for a blacksmith with the will to do the incredible.

He also knew that California had to teach the whites and the colored to agree. None of them could be moved now. It is first and foremost the upbringing which creates a person's attitude. No more blood was to flow in his republic, Nataqua. Peter walked determinedly into his forge to find some things: tools, bridles, horsehoes, axes, knives, and everything he had hidden away in the corners. He also found all his blankets and loaded everything on a couple of horses. All alone he rode out to the Washoe camp. It was evening when he got there. There was a pause in the battle because the whites had withdrawn. Some of them went home to water their animals. The ones that were left look surprised at Peter Lassen. None of them dared say anything to him, because he had a distant and secluded expression on his face.

He could hear the drums from their camp, and he could see many bonfires in the twilight. Peter was not afraid for his life. He did not believe that any Indian would kill him—at least not here in Honey Lake Valley. They knew him. He was the first white person who settled here. They knew that he would not kill and he was not unreliable about his agreements. The Indians were excited now, he could hear. If they should happen to kill him . . . yes, one day it might happen—one day everything would be over. Everything is change. The child he saw yesterday was a little changed today. It had learned something since yesterday. The eyes have gotten a different expression, the nails have grown and the hair also. Nothing in life is at ease. Even he himself would one day be gone.

Peter had never participated much in the church or its ministry, but here he was on his way into the emotional Indian camp getting a curious thought. Imagine if there was eternal life? Imagine that he, one place or another here on earth or outside of it, in eternity should sit and watch, how his house here in Honey Lake Valley fell into decay, became old, and some day fell apart from old age. Imagine that he in eternity should witness that the valley became overpopulated, maybe destroyed by golddiggers. Imagine that he from eternity should watch the small children . . . whom he daily says "hello" to, become old, wrinkled, worn out, sick, and one day die. What if the whole earth disappeared one day? And this he had to watch sitting in eternity without being able to do anything. He who had loved everything new, all the places where no man had ever set foot before. No, then it would be better anyway if there was no eternal life. The eternity, which his childhood vicar Henrich Kampmann in Farum had spoken so much about, did not seem very appealing to Peter.

Another thought also came to him—his mother, sister, and brother. Why hadn't he ever written to them? All of a sudden he felt guilty. Why in the world did he not ever send them a letter? Maybe his mother was dead? Maybe his sister also? His brother, yes, he didn't even know where he lived. A new thought came into his mind. *What about all my belongings?* He was thinking about his land. He also owned land outside the valley. He was a rich man, but without heirs. Maybe he should at some time make a will. Who would inherit his land?

All the people he had known in the course of time were gone—dead or gone to other places. All of a sudden he felt a deep longing for a good friend.

With this longing in his mind he rode into the camp with his two horses after him.

The dancing warriors did not notice him. He found the chief's tent and asked an old Indian to keep an eye on his horses. He walked into the tent, the chief was not alone. He knew the Washoe chief, because he had met him several times and spoken with him. He was very young and apparently had no hold on his warriors.

"Big Chief," Peter said, even though he did not feel that this form of address was appropriate. However, he did not want to lose control of the situation now. "I come to you as a friend and the Indian agent. I am to make sure that you Indians do not suffer from injustice."

The Washoe chief seemed a little shy. He was a coward and felt uneasy at Peter's secure manners. He made an uncertain movement with the one hand and hinted that Peter sit down.

Peter sat down on a bunch of hides close to the fire. "Big Chief," he repeated, "this war you will never win. The whites in the valley have sent a message to the governor for help. Do you know what *help* means? Soldiers!"

There was a moment's silence in the tent. The sound of drums and dancing feet penetrated into the tents and created a tense atmosphere. *Yes, yes,* Peter thought, *the Washoe warriors are happy right now. They are without worries in their ecstasy. They don't think about anything at all. They would probably not even notice if they were attacked right this minute.*

"I have tools outside on my horses. It is things you have use for. I also brought paper and pen so we can write a peace treaty," Peter said seriously and looked at the closed Indian face across from him by the fire.

It was hot in the tent, and the chief here also refused to wear the white people's clothes. He was only wearing a loincloth made of leather. Peter appealed to him: "The soldiers mean no more Washoes. The soldiers mean burned-down tents. No more squaw and children."

The chief suddenly got an interested gleam in his dull eyes.

Peter nodded and said, "Shall I get my bags?"

While he fetched his saddlebags, the Washoe chief summoned some of his warriors. Some old curious Indians were also coming. Peter unpacked. Apparently they were most interested in the axes and knives, but they also wanted to have blankets. The Indians liked the white people's soft blankets very much. It gave a high status to wear blankets around the shoulders when it was a little chilly. While they looked at the contents of the saddlebags, Peter found some paper and an ink bottle. He had from time to time written a few letters and documents, but he was a little uncertain about the way the treaty should be made. He began by writing the date at the top and, after that, between which persons the treaty would be valid. Then he wrote on, that the Washoe Indians hereby desist from making war against the whites in Honey Lake Valley at the receipt of the tools and blankets he brought with him.

The dancing warriors had become aware that something unusual was going on in the chief's tent. One after the other they came sneaking in, and when there was room for no more, the rest of them stood outside. Peter read his peace treaty out loud. The chief would not sign—a greedy look had entered his eyes.

"Okay, Big Chief, then take my one horse also," Peter said reluctantly.

The chief put two fingers up. "Two horses, and I sign."

Peter screwed up his clear blue eyes. "You get the two horses if you sign that you not only end this war, but also promise never more to make war against the whites. In return I promise you that you will never more be attacked by the whites."

The chief nodded satisfied, and Peter added a few lines to the peace treaty. The chief signed with a squiggle, and Peter wrote the chief's name. Peter also signed, and the chief was satisfied. A short moment later a worried look came into his narrow little nervous face, while he whispered, "No soldiers," and he stood in front of Peter. Peter looked at the skinny brown person and noticed that the chief was not much taller than himself.

"No soldiers," Peter said. "Tomorrow you move some distance away. I will talk with Maidu and Paiute."

The chief nodded, and Peter shook hands the American way. Then he fought his way out from the crowded tent with his empty saddlebags. He looked at his two well-groomed horses with a last loving look, but decided not to feel too bad about the loss. It was him, Peter Lassen from Denmark, who was the Indian agent, and no one was to send after help from the outside without first having asked him. Peter could handle the Indians himself, because this was his republic. He rode home in the black California night. The horse's hooves found the paths in the dark, because the Indian agent was lost in deep thought.

A couple of days after Peter had made his peace treaty with the Washoe Indians, Old Winnemucca and his son John came to Peter Lassen's house. John always acted as an interpreter for his father at special formal occations.

Winnemucca was dressed in full chief vesture. Peter received them outside his big log house and greeted them with great respect. Then he showed them inside. Peter Lassen's living room was something special. He had made all the furniture himself. They were beautifully made and done with great accuracy. In the middle of the floor was a large table. The open fireplace in the wall was so big that it could hold cordwood.

On the wall hung the clock and his father's pipe. That was all that he had kept from the things he brought with him from Denmark a long time ago. The clock still worked. Everytime it stopped, he cleaned and repaired it with the utmost care.

Besides Winnemucca and his son, K. J. Williams and Isaac Roop were also present.

Peter put his tobacco out, and very slowly the conversation began. Winnemucca knew Peter, and he realized that Peter was very keen to get all the hostilities ended before the governor's soldiers arrived.

The chief also wanted to end the war, as the Washoe tribe had pulled out of the fight.

"Washoe warriors are cowards. They were never able to fight," he said with contempt. He looked at Peter and continued, "What will you give us, Old Peter Lassen?" Winnemucca felt his strength. The whites shall not get peace for nothing.

Isaac Roop winked his eye at Peter and handed the chief the list of things, a list they had put together yesterday.

Winnemucca and his son discussed it between themselves, and they were not completely satisfied. They wanted more on the list. Now, when they could not make war anymore, they wanted an ample supply of blankets to elevate their prestige. They also wanted some combs and thimbles. It all took time, but finally after many hours of negotiations, they reached an agreement and got the peace treaty signed.

Honey Lake Valley
the fifth of January 1858
Treaty written the fifth day in January one thousand eight hundred and fifty-eight (1858) between the chief of the Smoke Creek Group of the Paiute tribe, by the name of Winnemucca, and P. Lassen, Isaac Roop, and J. Williams, underagents of J. T. Henley, superintendent for Indian matters in California.

P. Lassen, Isaac Roop, and J. Williams agree to give Winnemucca, chief of the Paiute Indians, the clothing and wool blankets, provided by J. T. Henley on the conditions he has outlined.

Winnemucca, chief of the Paiute Indians at Smoke Creek, agrees, in consideration of the clothing and wool blankets, et cetera, he has received, to keep peace with the whole population in Honey Lake Valley and the surroundings and also to refrain from stealing cattle and from any other kind of theft from the whites in the aforementioned area and to return, to the extent that he is able, all cattle stolen from them, and he agrees further that all supplies to him from the whites and all connections with these shall cease, if he is not able to fulfill his part of the treaty.

     J. Williams
     P. Lassen
     I. Roop

     underagents

     [Winnemucca, chief of
     Smoke Creek Group
     of the Paiute Indians,
     left his mark]

When the governor's soldiers reached Honey Lake Valley, there was not one single Indian in the area.

  Peter Lassen received the soldiers politely and made sure that they were taken care of in the best way. He regretted that they had been called way up here to the valley, but the small Indian riot that had taken place wasn't worth mentioning.

  "In Honey Lake Valley we deal with our own affairs."

Twenty

Peter was standing in the door of his house looking toward the mountains. It was late in the afternoon, and he felt a strange weakness in his body. The clock ticked on the wall, and a good heat emanated from the fireplace. In a little while he would heat up his soup and go to bed.

Tomorrow he could be a dead man. Well, fifty-eight years was a good age. He had known many who never reached that age. Nevertheless, he wanted to live a little longer.

He and his neighbor Alfred Smith traveled to Peter's old ranch by Stone Creek to quarry millstones, because there was a need for one more mill there in the valley. It was so fertile, and there was so much grain—much more than one single mill could handle.

Peter knew where the millstones were, and it was easy to cut them. On the way home it was difficult for them to get the heavily laden wagon over a hill. Hines and Dr. Spalding happened to come by with the freight wagon. Dr. Spalding was along to pick up his drugstore merchandise. They tried to help. Peter walked behind the wagon with a stone, ready to put it behind one of the wagon's rear wheels if it should start sliding backwards. But suddenly a chain broke, and the wagon started rolling down. Peter fell and dropped the stone, but by a stroke of good luck, the stone fell in such a way that it stopped the wagon. Otherwise the heavy wagon would have rolled over him.

Peter had often been close to death in his eventful life, but this time the incident made him sad. He had a strange feeling that this was an omen about his death. Peter could sense that something strange had come into his life.

He had gotten the millstones home, but now he had a feeling that he would never see the finished mill.

There were rumors going around that silver had been found in the Black-Rock Canyon. Peter had immediately talked to Weatherlow, Latorp, Kitte, Jameson, Wyatt, and Clapper about making an expedition to the place to find out if this was true. It was also a question of whether it was worthwhile to mine silver.

Until now, Peter had not been especially lucky with his gold mining, so maybe his luck was in silver.

He sighed and felt very lonely. He had become a wealthy man and was frequently mentioned in magazines and newspapers. He was becoming a myth, but nevertheless he had always been missing the most essential thing—love, that peace of mind that another human being can offer. A myth? What could he use that for?

The silver was a new challenge, and this was the way it was with him, new challenges made him forget his sensitive yearning.

Strange how the sun's warm, friendly fingers always leave a little lonesome coolness. At noon, when the sun is highest in the sky, it is already giving warning about the afternoon's long oblique beams, gliding lonely over the mountains, making the snow-covered mountain peaks more distant, still more impossible to reach.

He thought on; the sun, the light, our source of life, leaves a cool residue of sadness and unfulfilled dreams. Perhaps true companionship is an illusion. It does not exist. You believe you are together with others in a task. We can hunt together. We can light a fire. We can fight together, dig for gold together, eat together, but you are always really alone. You can see the prints of the horses' hooves leading away from you in the dry soil. You can see the place where they slept

by the fire, but when they are gone, you are by yourself again.
 You can feel uncertain yearning, remember pieces of talks, remember their smell, but you can never really bring them along with you out in the desert. They live for a while inside you, and then they are gone. It happens that you meet them again later and they have become quite different from the way you remember or you have become different and cannot understand what it was that once brought you together. It also happens that you become really excited to see somebody again, but in the excitement lies also the pain and the feeling that the meeting has become just a meeting, or that the one you saw again did not feel the same kind of excitement.
 He sighed a little at this thought—all the pieces of the human puzzle running around in his mind. He could not hold on to them. No one lives within him any more, not one has found rest in his soul, none whom he can meet in the sun's searching morning hands, when he wakes up tired from those nights filled with pain and inner turmoil. Those mornings his body was reluctant and without happiness. This kind of poverty was the worst.
 He had gained everything without really caring about it. He had always wanted power but it had been handed to him as a square and unpleasant mailbag that had to be delivered in just the right way. He had always sought the impossible, which seemed to be further out in the cool evasive afternoon sunbeams. All his life he sought brotherhood and unity; he founded Masonic lodges wherever he went. All the glory and honor he received never really penetrated into his consciousness. It was somebody else they wrote and talked about, because he was still deepest down the boy who ran barefoot and lonely in the fields around Farum. Always on his way, always full of hope that one or another would reach out his hand and give him a friendly pat on the head, but it never happened. At that time he had sworn that he would never be poor and

lonely. He had made a lot of money, but he had never been able to defeat loneliness, and now he was seeking it himself.

It was a cool day with a light breeze running through the big pine trees that grew around his house. While the wind played gently with the branches of the trees, he thought that the unity he had always sought and hoped for was merely a dream. Reality was the trees, the sun, the wind, his old dog, and his horse; the battles in the mountains and the frost that bit his fingers. All that had been reality. A human being is only alive right there, where he is standing. Everything else is like a reflection coming and going in a turbulent spring river. Everything is pictures, pictures in changing, pictures on their way, not to be held on to.

The world, always tempting him in his conscience behind the bluish and blurred forest of his mind, had been dissolved—it was not there anymore. He had become an old man. He looked up at the mountains and caught a glimpse of the California condor circling unaffectedly over the treetops.

Twenty-one

On April 17, 1859, Weatherlow, Latorp, Kitte, and Jameson departed, destined for the western shore of Lake Pyramid. On April 19, Clapper, Wyatt, and Peter also made for the west shore of Lake Pyramid. They agreed that it would be easier to travel in two groups. The mountains were impassable, and if too many traveled together, the result would often be that members of the party got separated along the way. Peter had worked out that there must be about 140 miles to Black-Rock Canyon.

Clapper and Wyatt were mature men, just like Peter. Wyatt was close on sixty years, and Peter had been a bit concerned at the idea of having him along on the trip. The fact was that he was overweight, and Peter knew that he could not cope with the hardships very well.

Clapper was about fifty years old and in considerably better form. Peter had Clapper look after the pack mules.

Peter rode his usual horse. By now it was twelve years old, but it was still good for riding in the mountains. Wyatt rode a very fine thoroughbred. It was nervous and shy. Peter could not help but be a little sorry for the poor beast that had to carry that big mountain of flesh.

On Sunday, April 24, Peter and his traveling companions reached the appointed place by Black-Rock Canyon. However, they could not find the other four and so decided to wait a few days. It could be that they would turn up soon.

On Monday, Clapper rode to Mud Lake to look for the others.

Wyatt and Peter remained in the camp to fix a few things. Wyatt walked about uneasily at the outskirts of the camp and thought. He looked like one who was waiting for something. The big stout man with the small piggy eyes and the fleshy nose, whose tip almost touched the broad bluish lips, was evidently up to something. He was thinking about what happened yesterday.

Peter was busy making his arrangements for the night, and the late afternoon sunbeams gave a rose tint to the mountain peaks. Wyatt had promised to gather plenty of firewood so that the fire could burn through the night. While he went about raking the thicket close to the camp, he found something that almost made him lose his breath. In a rock wall there was a well-concealed entrance to a mine. The scrub was close, and it looked as if the place had been abandoned for many years. The entrance to the mine was covered with several boulders, and the scrub had grown up in front of it. More than usual acuteness was required to find the place. It was a stroke of luck that he had found it in this way. He removed the large rocks and discovered that the gallery was full of silver—silver that had been mined, shaped, and stacked; ready to move. There was far more silver here than it was possible to find at those places in Black-Rock Canyon that had already been checked.

This place was abandoned, and the man, or men, who used to mine the silver had disappeared. Perhaps they had found silver or gold at another location, or else they had died, killed by Indians many years ago.

Wyatt had been standing for a long time staring at his wholly inestimable find. Here was the treasure he had been dreaming about all his life. He visualized his long wearisome life passing in review—the toilsome years as a farmer and as a goldminer in California. He had always hoped and believed that one day he would find something that could change his course of life—something that would make his life different and great. Now he faced it. He had attained the object of his dreams. When he had enjoyed the situation for a while, a thought dawned upon him. He had come up here together with two others, and it was planned that the party was to be joined by a further four men in the course of a few days. That meant that there would be seven to share the silver.

Even though there was silver at Black Rock, it was quite evident that this mine had not been opened recently. If he could get the two from his own traveling party, and also the four others, engaged in searching for other sources, he could keep the mine secret. Then he could sell the silver on the sly, become a rich man, and one day move to new parts of the country.

It was clear, however, that his six traveling companions would demand their share if they got wind of his mine. In particular, the officious Peter Lassen would be difficult. With his usual charity, he would undoubtedly insist that the money be spent on some new building or industrial undertaking at Honey Lake Valley. Everything that Peter dealt with had to be for the benefit of others. Obviously, the Dane did not like it that people merely scraped money together for their own consumption. Altogether, Wyatt was often tired of this well-rounded man who poked his nose into everything. Added to this, people looked up to the unimpressive man. He was the king of Honey Lake. Even the most troublesome Indian tribes obeyed him.

Peter Lassen was asked for advice about all sorts of things. There was no practical problem that he could not solve. Wyatt tried to crawl a short distance into the gallery to enjoy his find, but his corpulence prevented him from getting in very far. While he crawled out of the gallery, panting and out of breath, he heard unmistakable steps among the boulders near the mine.

He tried to keep as quiet as a mouse and to refrain from

panting too loudly, but it was too late. He saw Peter's friendly face by the gallery. Peter squatted and looked into the passageway.

"So, it's you, Wyatt! What a find we have made, eh?"

Wyatt noticed at once that Peter said "we." The battle was lost. He would not be in a position to count on full proceeds from the mine now.

"How on earth did you find me here?" Wyatt asked glumly.

"Well, I thought there was something about the place here, and besides, I could hear you as well." Peter sounded in good form and was beyond all measure pleased with the large silver cache. He crawled all the way into the gallery, and looked at the silver blocks, and he immediately established that there was an incredible quantity of silver.

Wyatt stood outside in the meanwhile, and asked himself why on earth he was dogged by misfortune. Why could he alone never get away with anything? Why could he never succeed at anything? While he was standing in the thicket waiting for Peter, he saw some Indians higher up on the mountain. He could not quite make out which tribe they belonged to, but he took it for granted that they were friendly.

Peter came out again. They carefully closed the mine with the boulders and straightened the scrub a little in front of the entrance. The whole thing should look as untouched as ever.

"It will soon be dark," Peter said. "I must hurry back to the camp. It would be unfortunate for us if the Indians stole our equipment. Besides, maybe Clapper has come back."

"Okay, I'm coming in a moment," Wyatt mumbled.

Peter disappeared with all possible speed down the graveled path among the conifers.

Wyatt stood looking after him and wondered that the little man of almost sixty was such a good walker.

Twenty-two

Now Wyatt stood looking up the mountain and noted that the Indians from yesterday had turned up again, apparently to make contact with him.

There was something dark and obscure within him that kept him from calling Peter or Clapper, who had returned late last night.

Wyatt looked closer at the little band of Indians approaching. They looked somewhat like Paiutes but he was not quite sure. The leader of the party was especially indeterminable.

Wyatt knew a little Shoshonean, the language of the Paiutes, and he tried to question them as to what they wanted. After some palavering, he understood that they wanted bullets for their guns. They pointed to their firearms and with many gestures made it clear that they had run out of ammunition. Wyatt could not make them disclose to which tribe they belong.

He tried again and again to make himself understood in Shoshonean. Then a peculiar thought occurred to him. What if Peter and Clapper did not return from this expedition? If, for instance, they were to perish by an accident, or be killed by the Indians, well then, he would indeed be the only person to know about the mine. Then he could mine the silver and cart it away, sell it, and get the whole profit for himself. He could buy land at a different place. He could become a rich and free man. He explained to the Indians that they could come along to the camp and get bullets, but there were conditions. They would only get the ammo if they would do him a favor. Namely, they were to shoot the two other men in the camp. Yet it was obvious that they would have to do it from an ambush.

He explained to the Indians that the two men, both the short gray-haired one and the tall dark-haired man, were crack shots, so they must take pains to hit them the first time they shoot.

The Indians were somewhat astonished but apparently they understood. Suddenly they ran up the mountain, while they discussed the strange proposition amongst themselves.

Wyatt walked slowly down the gravel track toward the camp. It was almost dark now, and the branches of the coniferous trees swept the ground in silent movements. In his mind there was darkness. He felt a strangely heavy and relentless pain in his abdomen—a sensation that nauseated him.

When he got out of the soft darkness of the conifers, he caught sight of the light from the campfire. He heard voices in the quiet evening, and he knew that Clapper and Peter were talking about the silver mine.

He could smell roasted meat. He was both hungry and tired, but he felt a curious urge to go back to the conifers and hide in their murky shadows, fuse with the night, become lost in something soft and eternal. Meanwhile, his tired legs continued their walk toward the camp, where he sat down heavily by the fire.

Sure enough, they were speaking about the great silver find. The chat around the campfire was animated. Peter roasted venison and expatiated on the ways the great sum of money they would now gain might be applied in Honey Lake Valley.

Clapper had not found the slightest trace of the other four, and they entertained the possibility that they might have lost their way or that the Indians might have assaulted them. Peter could hardly believe the latter, for there were no hostile

Indians hereabouts. After the last great uprising when they had signed treaties with both Washoe and Paiute, there had not been the least hint of unrest.

When the meat had become tender, they ate in silence and drank a touch of California wine with it.

The night was mild and the stars twinkled high in the sky, smiling down on the lofty mountain peaks. The fire crackled; Peter had provided an ample supply of wood so that it might burn overnight.

Now and again, Peter cast a sidelong glance at Wyatt. He was surprised that the big fat man did not eat very much of the savory meat. Peter had roasted plenty, though, because he knew the ravenous appetite of his traveling companion. It was as if Wyatt were incessantly waiting for something, and he avoided the prying look Peter gave him.

Soft footsteps were heard in the scrub. Clapper and Peter instinctively grabbed their guns, and suddenly he was there. They could only spy the outline of him behind the fire in the gentle night. In shaky Shoshonean, he asked for bullets. Peter tried to form an impression of him, but he could only make out his naked body in the dark. The man wore a loincloth of hide and his black hair was plaited.

"Don't give him any bullets," said Clapper warningly.

Peter looked in the direction of Wyatt, who was remarkably quiet and carefully avoided looking at either of them.

"Oh well, do let him have a few shots," Peter said in a fatherly voice. He was an Indian agent, and he knew what the Indians should or should not have. Peter could not tolerate others meddling in his affairs in regard to the Indians. He got up and found his game bag. He took a handful of bullets, walked back to the fire, and extended his hand with the bullets toward the Indian. The latter quickly bent forward and received the ammunition. Just then, the glow from the fire caught the Indian's face, and a flash of recognition flitted through Peter's consciousness. He had seen this Indian before. The native looked at him; for a fraction of a second their eyes met over the fire. The Indian kept a straight face, but Peter knew that he recognized him. He was the Yana Indian who one day long ago had thrown himself as a living torch into the river, when Frémont and Kit Carlson's men murdered his tribal kinsmen by Benton City. The Indian had then sworn vengeance upon Peter, who now felt a cold current in his fingertips as the bullets slid from his hand onto the hard-bitten palm of the Indian.

He was away on soundless moccasins.

"Everyone knows Uncle Pete," said Peter with an assumed air.

Clapper made a round to see if the animals were well tethered for the night.

All three went to sleep. None of them thought of keeping watch. Why? They were in the land of the Paiutes, and here they felt safe. Still, there was a slight uneasiness in Peter's heart, for he knew that there was in any case one Indian in this vicinity who did not belong to the Paiutes, and he was the Yana that he himself had just given a handful of bullets.

Twenty-three

A reddish gold border gradually formed about the mountain peaks, a sign that the sun was about to bring daytime to Black Rock Canyon. The stillness was broken by a solitary chirp from a bird here and there in the tall conifers. The creek down at the bottom of the valley purled cautiously and apologetically over the many stones and rough passages. There was a cool devout tranquility before the light and the day broke in earnest. Peter and Clapper were soundly asleep in their leather bags by the extinct fire.

Wyatt sat heavy with sleep and tried to crawl out of his sleeping bag. He looked confused and tired—a man left between dream and reality. He looked toward the peaks, and suddenly he thought that the rose-pink shadows lining the mountain were growing venomously yellow, more so as the light gained power.

With some effort he got to his feet and hitched his pants and his closefitting jacket into proper position.

Again he looked at the mountains and caught sight of something—Indian profiles against the breaking light. The clear-cut profiles were surrounded by a luminous aura. He looked astonished at the strange sight. It was all too silent and unreal around him. Then the shot rang out! He stood motionless on the spot and looked toward the bright mountains. At last he turned his head to his two traveling companions. Clapper lay quite still, but Peter stirred in his sleep, awakened by the shot.

Wyatt grabbed his gun and looked up at the Indians. Would there be more shots?

He was afraid to approach the two at the extinct fire until he knew if the shooting was over.

He wondered whether Clapper had been hit.

He looked at Clapper and understood that he was dead. What if they don't shoot any more? Could one rely on these Indians? He raised the gun and put the butt to his cheek. A shot rang out among the mountaintops. Another shot sounded; then all became still as the golden light from the mountains spread and gilt the evergreens on the hillsides.

Peter had had a bad night on the stony ground. He was awakened several times because his leg had rested too long on a stone edge and was asleep. He had the smell of burned tents and human skin in his nostrils. He saw the Indian out in the river, perceived his hatred and the vengefulness in his raised fists. He saw that the river was rough, but suddenly it turned quiet and smooth as a mirror. He lay on his stomach and looked into the clear water. He noticed gravestones down at the bottom, lots of gravestones with large inscriptions. But he could not read what it said on the many gravestones. Down at the bottom, among the stones, a little Indian boy was walking about. He wore only a loincloth. He was light brown and chubby. His black hair reached his shoulders. He turned his face upward and smiled on Peter. Suddenly it was no longer the boy who smiled, but Dove. "My son," mumbled Peter and tried to reach for the boy in the cool water.

A metallic sound woke him up. He turned in the sleeping bag and looked at Clapper. He was half out of his sleeping bag with his face pressed against the ground. Peter got up on one elbow, put his free arm around Clapper's shoulder, and lifted it a little. The face let go of its hold on the earth. Peter noted that pebbles and pine needles were stuck in the facial skin. Suddenly Clapper's temple burst like fragile china and the blood gushed out, warm red blood. Clapper looked at Peter with an empty and humble glance. "He is dead," mumbled Peter tonelessly.

Dead! Peter knew that he must hurry now. But he could not. His movements were leaden and he felt the ice-cold imminence of death. He got up on his knees and grabbed his gun. He wanted to gather his essential things and then run for his horse. He had hardly thought the word *horse* when he heard the sound of fleeing hooves. The horses had become frightened at the shots, and they had broken loose. It was as though his life were fleeing with them.

He stood up, shaded his eyes with his hand, and looked toward the rocks. From where did the shots come?

He felt betrayed. It could not be Paiutes, could it? Winnemucca was his friend. No, he could see the angry Yana Indian in his mind's eye. He had handed him the shots himself. He thought of Wyatt and turned his head to the opposite side. He opened his eyes wide in astonishment. Wyatt stood a few yards away, as still as a poker, with the gun butt put to his cheek. Peter looked straight into the barrel. A shot sounded from the mountain. Something smartingly merciless struck through his ribs into the chest. He looked at Wyatt's glazed eyes. "I've been hit," Peter whispered in surprise. He watched Wyatt's thick finger approach the trigger, and then yet another shot resounded among the hills.

Peter felt something tear into his neck. He dropped to the ground, flat on his face.

From a far-off horizon he could hear the sound of Wyatt's escaping steps. The warm blood gushed from him. He was like a defenseless wounded animal. He gazed down at the dry Californian soil. He had earth and ants in his eyes, but he had no vital power left to raise a hand.

The earth greedily drank his blood, his last sacrifice, his last act of kindness to the earth he loved; the earth he had traversed, length and breadth; the earth he had named, explored, loved, and taken possession of with the same curiosity with which a lover takes his bride into his arms.

While his heart's blood dripped into the California soil, a lobe of a green beech leaf brushed his torn chest—a lobe of a beech leaf from the great tree by Lake Farum; he used to crawl out on its large boughs, which good-naturedly gave way over the clear water. From this beech he had had a good view of the little village church and the white main building of Farum Manor.

He was thinking of Johan, of his mother, and suddenly, as a remote unreal thought, he wished that the vicar at Farum Church was telling the truth when he said that we would all meet with our dear ones at last—when the earthly life was at an end. *Wonder if he spoke the truth?* he thought, exhausted, and clutched the earth with both hands. He died with his hands buried deep in the Californian soil and with an astounded look in his eyes.

Those who later found his almost decomposed corpse wondered at this astounded expression, which still reigned in his features. He looked like a man who had witnessed his own murder.

In his hour of death, the lobe of a Danish beech leaf had brushed his mind, but he died with both hands buried deep **in the California soil.**

Twenty-four

Wyatt fled. He ran and accidentally shot himself through one trouser leg. He could not find any horses, but after a while, miraculously, his black racehorse came running toward him.

The sorely tried animal must have nourished an inexplicable loyalty toward its overweight master—or was it simply bewildered? At any rate, it came toward him and let itself be caught. Wyatt rode full gallop the whole stretch to Susanville. The horse became a jade after that ride, and Wyatt a silent and quiet man.

Never once did he take the trouble to visit his precious silver mine at Black Rock Canyon.